The Would-Be Medium

My Ten-Year Journey as a Workshop Junkie

RENA HUISMAN

BALBOA.
PRESS

A DIVISION OF HAY HOUSE

Balboa Press books may be ordered through booksellers or by contacting:

Balboa Press
A Division of Hay House
1663 Liberty Drive
Bloomington, IN 47403
www.balboapress.com
1 (877) 407-4847

Because of the dynamic nature of the Internet, any web addresses or
links contained in this book may have changed since publication and
may no longer be valid. The views expressed in this work are solely those
of the author and do not necessarily reflect the views of the publisher,
and the publisher hereby disclaims any responsibility for them.

The author of this book does not dispense medical advice or prescribe the use
of any technique as a form of treatment for physical, emotional, or medical
problems without the advice of a physician, either directly or indirectly. The
intent of the author is only to offer information of a general nature to help
you in your quest for emotional and spiritual well-being. In the event you use
any of the information in this book for yourself, which is your constitutional
right, the author and the publisher assume no responsibility for your actions.

Any people depicted in stock imagery provided by Thinkstock are models,
and such images are being used for illustrative purposes only.
Certain stock imagery © Thinkstock.

Print information available on the last page.

ISBN: 978-1-5043-4526-2 (sc)
ISBN: 978-1-5043-4528-6 (hc)
ISBN: 978-1-5043-4527-9 (e)

Library of Congress Control Number: 2015919098

Balboa Press rev. date: 01/07/2016

This book is dedicated to the authors and instructors who led me out of the metaphysical and supernatural darkness and into the light. I wasn't crazy after all.

Contents

Preface

I started writing this book at the end of 2014. Coincidentally, that time marked the ten-year anniversary of when I took my first mediumship class. I had just finished reading another book about a famous medium and that person's path to fame and fortune when I thought, *There really should be a book about the rest of us frustrated students who have taken countless classes but haven't done anything professionally yet.*[1] So I wrote this book.

What follows is a collection of my experiences attending classes, taking courses, and enrolling in weekend workshops in an attempt to find answers. They were the stepping-stones necessary to understand and work with my psychic and mediumship abilities.

My journey began when I was thirty-eight and ended when I was forty-eight (2004–2014). Although it was not easy, it was well worth every dollar, tear, headache, hangover, temper tantrum, and keg of Miller Lite.

There were several times I gave up, lost faith, blamed God

---

[1] When I use the term *professional*, I am referring to a medium/psychic/healer who is paid for his or her services (such as readings or healings), considers such work his or her full- or part-time employment, can be contacted for an appointment, and/or teaches classes in his or her area of expertise for a fee. This is my way of separating a professional in the field from someone who gives readings for free to friends and family.

for leading me down the wrong path, and blamed my guardian angels and spirit guides for not doing their jobs. I didn't want to keep wasting my money on so many classes if I wasn't going to use what I learned professionally. It felt like high school chemistry and algebra—information I learned but never use. I figured that the divine had me confused with some other woman, and I wanted out. But it wasn't that easy.

What I learned is that you can't turn off that yearning to learn, to find answers to your questions, and to connect to the other side. It doesn't go away. It is patient, which I know nothing about. It sat there waiting in the corners of my mind until once again, I reached for a new book, searched for new a class, or took out my trusty deck of tarot cards. And then I went off again in search of a way to use what I already knew and to learn more.

All the names of the people in this book have been changed with the exception of my family members and the instructors. I made these changes to protect the privacy of my fellow students and to avoid lawsuits.

This book is written from my perspective and recollection of each event. If you believe that you recognize one of the classes and think that I have things out of order, or recall an event incorrectly, I apologize. Ultimately, this is my memoir based on my memory, which can get a little hazy sometimes. Enjoy!

Introduction

Growing up, I loved the movie *The Wizard of Oz*. Glinda the Good Witch was my idol. She was beautiful, calm, nurturing, and dressed in the most magnificent pink goddess gown I had ever seen. I believed in magic completely, wholeheartedly, without a doubt. No one ever talked about magic in my home, but that didn't matter, because I knew magic was real. I felt the same way about ghosts.

These topics were never discussed at home, partly because being brought up Catholic meant that my family automatically aligned ghosts with the devil. Therefore, any conversation about seeing strange things, hearing voices, or by some horrible chance, seeing something move was disregarded as an overactive imagination that needed to be stopped or the devil would come to get us. I can still hear my nine-year-old thoughts like it was yesterday.

"So let me get this straight, Mom; you are saying that if I see a ghost or hear voices in the house, it's all in my head. And if I can't get those things out of my head or stop seeing or hearing those things, the devil is going to come and get me?" Needless to say, there were no good options. So I did what most kids did back then: I stopped talking about it.

The exception to this rule was with my older brother, Peter. He was incredibly smart, did well in school, had plenty of friends, and was very attractive. I was the complete opposite of Peter. I was an awkward, tall, skinny chick with a big head of hair. Plus, I hated to read, so that was a major obstacle as well.

Peter was patient. He never questioned what I saw, heard, or felt. If I had a vision or a dream, he would listen and keep an eye out for anything that might be a premonition. We both loved the possibilities of the unknown, and over the years, we held séances with our cousins and the neighbor kids. It is interesting to look back and realize that it was a kind of movement. All of us were brought up in religious families, but we knew that there was something more out there. We couldn't put a finger on it, but we were crazy enough to try.

There are a few memories[2] in particular that still stick out after all these years. When I look back, there are dozens of strange things that have happened over my lifetime, but those took place before I knew what was happening. They occurred before I began to study metaphysics. I believe they were my lightbulbs, my "ah-ha" moments, confirmation that there was more to life than met the eye. They are what put me on this path in the first place, but it wasn't until 2003 that my journey began.

I was living in Mesa, Arizona, at the time. My husband, Kurt, and I had just divorced. We remained close as the kids went back and forth between our homes each Sunday. Our daughter, Sydney, chose the schedule; she said it gave her and her little brother, Travis, time to settle in and enjoy a full week with each parent before they had to switch again.

During the weeks that I didn't have the kids, I found that I had a lot of free time. This was a blessing and a curse. But it was mostly a curse because I had the time to do all of the things that I said I never had time for, which I found out was overeating and drinking. I longed for the voices of my children and some sense of normalcy. And yes, I even missed Kurt.

---

[2] See Appendix: My Early Memories.

It had been decades since I'd played with the Ouija board. And it had been almost as long since I'd intentionally done anything that would be considered metaphysical or paranormal—the one exception was when I bought a set of tarot cards on clearance from a local bookstore years earlier.

The cards were a little larger than a standard deck; they were about the same size as the average oracle cards you see today. They weren't menacing to look at; they displayed pictures of wheat on the outside and swords, coins, cups, and rods on the inside. It took weeks for me to decide to take them out of the original packaging. When I finally did, I was terrified that I would release the devil or some other sort of evil into our home just by touching them. Kurt, on the other hand, was very supportive and encouraged me to give them a try. He was obviously not Catholic.

The truth was, I had been eyeing them for weeks, walking around the same sales rack by the cash registers. Eventually, curiosity had won out, and I had finally broken down and bought them.

When I used them the first time, Kurt and I were still married and I was sitting on our bed. I read through the instruction booklet that was provided, shuffled the deck several times, and laid the cards out according to the picture in the booklet. It was my first tarot card spread.

It felt awesome. *I finally did it!* I was a fortune-teller, a gypsy, the person at the swap meet who charged ten dollars for a fifteen-minute reading. I'm not sure what I expected, but it was definitely not the stone-cold silence that surrounded me. I looked at the cards laid out on the bed, and they looked back at me. Then *nothing*. I opened the booklet and read through the meaning of each card, which seemed daunting. *Where is the magical information that is supposed to come to me automatically? Do I really have to memorize the meaning of each card?* The thought was overwhelming. I played with my deck for a few minutes longer, and then I put them away in a small, cloth pouch that I found in my end table drawer.

As the days went on, I wondered how playing with tarot cards could affect me and my family. Old fears started to surface again, which led to my deck spending several years waiting in the bottom drawer.

Still, I kept feeling this pull to go back to my cards. I took them out of their little pouch several times when the kids were with Kurt, but I knew I needed some guidance and answers to the dozens of questions flying around in my head. There was a metaphysical bookstore close by called Vision Quest. I had been there before for a reading when I was still married. I figured that, if anyone could help me with my confusion, it was someone in that store.

Finally, one Saturday afternoon, I drove over there. They had a good selection of books on various metaphysical subjects such as mediumship (communication between entities in the spirit world and those in the physical world), psychic awareness, psychometry (reading an object by touching or holding it), and tarot cards, but I didn't know where to begin.

As I looked around the room, I thought, *Maybe getting a reading is a good place to start.* Consequently, I booked an appointment and wandered around the book section until I heard a woman's voice say, "Rena, I'm ready for you."

She looked nice enough. *No weird, creepy vibes,* I thought as I introduced myself and sat down for my reading.

The details of what was said that day are long gone, but I remember leaving there feeling a million times better. And soon thereafter, I developed a plan to become more educated. That included taking a few classes and buying some books to understand what being psychic or being a medium meant. I was told that the metaphysics section of Borders was a great place to start.

So there I was, standing in Borders, a place I pretty much never went unless I was buying a new calendar or some music. I walked over to the metaphysical book section that eventually became my second home. I was jumpy, wondering what people would think of me. *Do they know what the word* metaphysical *means?* I knew I had just found out. But I also couldn't say I had ever paid much attention to anyone hanging out in *this* area before.

It was like coming home, sitting there on the floor and looking through dozens of books that day. There were stacks of them lying all around me. But I only bought one. It was called *The Psychic Pathway* by Sonia Choquette.

It was a workbook that contained exercises to increase your intuition and psychic awareness over a twelve-week period of time. It provided practical explanations about what it meant to be psychic, where the information came from, and the ethics behind using psychic abilities with other people. I learned about working with the *Clair Senses*: clairvoyance (seeing), clairaudience (hearing), clairsentience (feeling), clairgustance (tasting), clairalience (smelling), and claircognizance (knowing). I also read about the chakras (the seven main energy centers) and the aura (the etheric energy bodies around us).

Simple exercises walked me through how to work with my guides and use tools for divination, such as the tarot, the I Ching, and the pendulum. It also explained the importance of meditation, energy clearing, and psychic protection. It was very interesting to learn all the ways that psychic information could be obtained or shared between people and objects (intentionally or unintentionally). That book was the first of a large collection that I still own today.

Over the next twelve weeks, I worked the program, slowly losing my fears and moving toward what would end up becoming a life passion. Several weeks later, I went back into Borders to look for a new book and found one by Doreen Virtue. I can't remember whether it was *Divine Guidance* or *Divine Prescriptions,* but I ended up reading both of them.

Sonia's workbook exercises opened me up to the idea that I was psychic and most likely a medium. I learned that I had chakras and an invisible energy body that surrounded me. She also explained the use of popular divination tools. Doreen's book opened me up to the angelic realm. The stories she collected from people who experienced divine intervention were fascinating.

Between the two authors, I gathered the knowledge that helped me finally put my fears to rest. I knew that the things I was experiencing—such as hearing voices, seeing people that weren't in the physical world, and feeling someone touch me when no one was there—were real. I wasn't making them up, and most importantly, I wasn't alone in this journey. I had many guides from different realms in different dimensions of time and space by my side. I just had to have faith and ask for assistance.

The authors also talked about the importance of consistent practice, which included meditation and journaling. Because I didn't have any friends who were psychics or mediums to practice with, I had to rely on local classes. The only ones I knew of at that time were at Vision Quest. I attended my first class there, which turned out to be a group reading, not an actual practice. It was also the first time I saw an aura.

The woman giving the group readings was explaining the importance of how to phrase a question as I wrote mine down on a piece of paper, rolled it up, and placed it into a bowl. (The little pieces of rolled-up paper are called *billets*.). While she was talking, the back of her head lit up like a ray of sunshine had engulfed her from her shoulders up. She was showered with golden-white light!

It took a while for me to understand what I was seeing; I just stared at her with my mouth hanging open. Even after all my studying about auras, I had a delayed reaction. But it was working: I was opening up. Unfortunately, my search for a development group in town was going nowhere. The good news was that I had time and a little money to take a class out of state. Therefore, I went back to Sonia and Doreen's websites to look for an opportunity. Finally, I found a promising conference in San Francisco, California, where they were both speaking. *Woo-hoo!*

What followed is my ten-year journey into the world of psychics, mediums, and healers. Yes, I would do it all over again—but the next time I would sprinkle in a little ghost hunting as well!

Making a Mystical Connection Conference

My journey began in April of 2004, when I attended my first conference: Making a Mystical Connection. It took place in San Francisco, California. It was a one-day event I had found on Doreen or Sonia's website. Because I don't remember which one it was, I'm giving them both credit for the find.

I was living in Arizona at the time, so I was able to get a cheap flight to California. I was so excited to go that I flew in the night before, ensuring that I wouldn't miss anything.

The conference took place at the beautiful Argent Hotel in downtown San Francisco, a venue with old-time charm, gold fixtures, marble floors, and enormous chandeliers. I loved it. The conference was held before the popular I Can Do It! conferences sponsored by Hay House today. All of it was completely new to me.

On the morning of the conference, I woke up thinking about my brother, Peter. He had lived in San Francisco with his partner, Andrew, for ten years before he passed away in 1995. He loved the city from the first time he visited family there with my grandfather at age fifteen. He enjoyed the city life, busy streets, tall buildings, shopping, and great food. For me, San Francisco *was* Peter, and I kept wondering whether he was there with me.

Because I was too shy to eat downstairs in the restaurant by myself, I ordered room service for breakfast. Afterward, I walked down to the main elevator that led to the conference room where the event was taking place.

It was incredible. For starters, the hotel felt grand and expensive; so, when I walked out of the elevator and into the conference area, I felt a bit intimidated—especially when I heard the hustle and bustle of the crowd, which sounded like an outdoor marketplace.

When I came around the corner, I saw a large area with tables stacked with books, tarot cards, CDs, jewelry, and other items. People were walking around and shopping. Most of them were women carrying tote bags filled with their new purchases.

As I walked farther into the area, I saw two sets of double doors on my right with people checking tickets. I decided to pass on the shopping and head inside.

Because I had ordered preferred seating, a woman led me toward the first few rows. "Pick an open seat in this area," she said. Still in awe from my surroundings, I nodded and quickly found an open chair.

It was a very large ballroom with several chandeliers hanging from the ceiling. The walls were decorated with gold highlights, and the carpet matched. There were hundreds of people sitting in dozens of rows of chairs that started in the back of the room and went right up to the front of the elevated stage. There was one main aisle that stretched down the middle.

I was sitting in the third row near the double doors. Even three rows back, I felt like I was practically leaning on the microphone. It felt like a concert with the large speakers set up on stands in the front and back of the room.

There was a permanent smile on my face as I anxiously awaited the medium's arrival. John Holland was scheduled first, and then Sonia, and then Gordon Smith, and finally Doreen. I didn't know who Gordon was, but I had heard of John. *I can't believe I am going to see Sonia and Doreen in person.* I felt like a groupie—I guess that was better than feeling like a stalker.

A woman went up on stage. The audience immediately got .

quiet, and all eyes were fixed on her as she began the sound check on the mic. The excitement grew as she shared the logistics (restrooms, lobby, water fountain, etc.) and reminded everyone about the book signing after the conference was over.

When she stepped down, the voice over the speakers completed the sound check just as the runners came out. These were the people who ran around the room providing wireless microphones to the audience members. And then the master of ceremonies took the stage and kicked off the conference. Unfortunately, I don't remember who it was. It could have been Louise Hay, but I don't remember for sure.

It was finally time to begin. The lights changed, the music started, and John Holland was introduced. He came bouncing down the aisle as if he were on *The Price Is Right*. He skipped up the stairs and landed on the stage. He was out of breath when he took the mic, but he began his introductions like that was just part of the plan.

He was a blast of energy. What I didn't expect was his larger-than-life Boston accent! His introduction was theatrical and hilarious; his hands were flying everywhere as he spoke. And then he started giving random readings to the crowd. He was spot on every time, and the energy in the room continued to rise. Even in the saddest cases, there was humor to help the healing process. I was hooked and made a mental note to buy his book.

Next, Sonia Choquette took the stage. She didn't walk down the aisle, because she was already standing on the side of the stage when she was introduced. She looked nervous—or maybe she was silently talking to her guides, but she was gently swaying side to side and looking down at her feet. I can't imagine how she felt as she looked out over the vast sea of faces. I believe John introduced her before he walked off stage.

Sonia was wearing a beautiful pink-and-white lei. She explained immediately that it was made for her by one of her students as a gift of appreciation and she was extremely proud to be wearing it. She was very well spoken, but her energy was very different from John's—less energetic and more serious.

As I watched her, starstruck, she asked everyone to stand up. We all looked at each other in confusion as we stood up. And then she said, "Everyone, turn to your right and place your hands on the shoulders of the person in front of you." We did. "Now give that person a nice massage."

The room roared with laughter as we gave complete strangers shoulder massages. And then she said, "Now stop, turn to your left, and repay the favor!" There was another burst of laughter as we followed her instructions.

Before Sonia began giving readings to the audience, she talked about her guides in depth, providing their names, the roles they played in her day-to-day life, and how they influenced her readings. Shortly after that, a young lady was led down the aisle to the front of the stage. She suffered from a mental disability and thanked Sonia for her recent assistance. Hers was a difficult life. Sonia walked off stage, took off the lei, and placed it around the young woman's neck gently. Then she said, "You are beautiful inside and out. You deserve to be wearing this. It is my gift to you." The young woman began crying as Sonia gave her a hug.

During the time Sonia was on stage, the energy in the room noticeably shifted up and down. The highs were good, but the lows made me want to run out and drink. I figured that was normal because so much emotion was involved.

Next on stage was Gordon Smith. Because I had no idea who he was, I had no idea what to expect. And then the sound of bagpipes came pouring out of the sound system. *Is that Scottish music?*

Out came Gordon Smith like a rock star! He wore a gigantic smile and a kilt. Yes, I said kilt. It was totally kick-ass. The energy in the room went through the roof with his wonderful Scottish accent and amazing sense of humor. The audience was consumed with laughter.

His readings were incredible. As with John, I was a fan for life and made a note to read his books. To this day, I feel incredibly lucky to have seen him in person at the very beginning of my journey. With some luck and space on my Visa card, I will visit Scotland to see him again in person.

The last one on stage was Doreen Virtue. Once again, I was immediately starstruck. She didn't walk down the aisle, because she was already on the stage. She was wearing one of her signature flowing goddess gowns and looked fabulous.

Doreen's energy was not serious like Sonia's, but it was not as light and airy as John's and Gordon's—it was somewhere in between. She spoke matter-of-factly, with a dry sense of humor. During her introduction, she explained the angelic realm, the archangels, and the ascended masters she works with. Later, she shared messages from them, reminding us that we were never alone. She also explained the symbolic guidance they provided via music, repetitive numbers, birds, butterflies, coins showing up in strange places (mostly pennies and dimes), feathers, and in our dreams.

She directed most of the messages to the entire group rather than to individuals, and the vibration in the room felt completely different from what we experienced with the first three mediums. It felt informative and uplifting, like listening to talk radio wrapped in jazz music.

After the show ended, Sonia and John were scheduled to sign books. I went out the double doors quickly and bought a copy of John's book *Born Knowing*. Because I didn't bring a book from home for Sonia to sign, I bought one of hers: *True Balance*.

After my purchase, I looked over and saw John sitting at his table with no one in line. Today, that would be a small miracle for sure. I walked over with my book and mumbled something like, "Um, hi. Can you sign this book?" He looked like he had a giant headache. "Sure, what is your name?" More coherently this time, I said, "Rena." He took out his black Sharpie and wrote, "Rena, all the best. JHolland." (I'm guessing on that last part because it looks like a J followed by some other letters.) I thanked him, held the book tightly against my chest, and walked toward the long line for

Sonia. *Oh my God. I am going to meet her in person, have a one-on-one conversation with her ... Well, kind of, anyway.*

I stood there trying not to faint. Sure, there were a couple of hundred people standing all around us, including the stalkers who were listening to what she was saying to everyone. *Creepy.* But to me, it was like a one-on-one.

As I stood in line, I started to lose my nerve and seriously thought about leaving. *What if I get up there and can't speak? Worse, what if I say something really stupid or forget my name?*

Then it was my turn. My nerves immediately went away when I noticed how tired she looked. *This must be divine intervention, because just two seconds ago I was going to throw up.* She wasn't crabby, but she seemed, in my humble opinion, really tired. She gave me a half smile, took my book, and asked for my name, which I managed to mumble out for the second time that day.

As I stood there silently watching her, she began to give me a mini-reading, something I did not expect. I have forgotten most of it over the years, but there was one part that continues to haunt me to this day: "You were not meant to be in the back row; you were meant to be up front, in the light. You need to stop hiding in the back row and be up front where you belong."

I froze, and my eyes bugged out because I knew exactly what she meant. What I didn't know was how dark it would be in that back row, and how being there would change my life forever. At that moment, I was at the beginning of my dark times, nowhere close to the end.

(Hey, Sonia, if by some chance you are reading this book, I send you a heartfelt *thank you* for that moment of inspiration. I felt special and important, something that I longed for. It helped me get through those years and realize that the light was there all along, as were the opportunities for me to step into it and feel worthy of it. This book is living proof.)

The conference marked the beginning of my travels. I'm still in shock that I had the nuts to sign up for it in the first place, not to mention travel there on my own. I will call it *divine persuasion.*

Also, I must mention that I think I had a visit from my brother, Peter. It was during the break, when I went to the main lobby to find something to drink. Oddly, I was the only one waiting at the elevator. The double doors opened, I walked in, and I pushed the button for the main lobby. Then a creepy vibe hit me, it felt like someone was watching me. The doors didn't close, so I pushed the button again. Nothing. And then they closed and opened again quickly. I held the doors open and looked out, expecting to see someone waiting, but there was no one there. And then the doors did the same thing again. At that point, it hit me: maybe Peter is saying *hi*. So I said aloud, "Hey, Peter, is that you?" And then the doors did it again! "I miss you too!" I said as they finally closed.

You are probably thinking it was just the elevator malfunctioning, but what are the odds of me being alone in the elevator for that long with all those people coming and going? And why would the elevator doors open and close so many times without anyone pushing the buttons on the other side? I'm just saying ...

The Mediumship Program
with Doreen Virtue

When I came home from the conference in San Francisco, the first thing I did was call Kurt. He had just moved to Tustin, California, the month before for a new job with a new financial institution. The kids and I missed him, but he was still relatively close for weekend visits. When he answered the phone, I told him every detail about the show, my personal experiences, and my even bigger need for answers. I'm sure I sounded like a rambling idiot, but Kurt was patient.

As we talked, I knew that in order to move forward, I had to spend more time with like-minded people. In 2004, that was not an easy task, so I went back to the mediums I had seen (and met) in person, Sonia and Doreen.

After checking on both of their websites, I found out that Sonia had a class in Chicago, which would add travel costs to the expense of tuition. Also, it was not scheduled for a long time: March 2005. Therefore, I decided to attend Doreen's mediumship program, which was scheduled in October at the Laguna Inn in Laguna Beach, California. All it required was a drive to California. There, I could drop the kids off with Kurt and sleep on his sofa in the evenings for free.

But in a weird twist of fate, by October of 2004, the kids were living with Kurt, and I was living alone in Arizona. They went over for summer vacation and decided to stay. It was heartbreaking, but I understood. So when the time came, Kurt was happy to have me stay over with him and the kids. Kurt is a really great guy that way.

I was up bright and early Saturday morning. Kurt was already awake, helping me decide what to wear and which freeway to take. I had spent the evening before hanging out with him and the kids. It was heaven, and I started the day in the greatest mood.

The class was a quick sixteen miles of interstate mixed with a gorgeous canyon road from Kurt's apartment. When I came out of the canyon, the Pacific Ocean was visible directly in front of me. The sun bounced off the waves, the seagulls swooped up and down. It was breathtaking. I turned right onto Pacific Coast Highway, and the hotel was on my left. It sat right on the sand. *Absolutely perfect,* I thought as I turned onto the driveway.

The hotel had three levels. Our class was held at the top, in a conference room with a view of the ocean on one side and a patio off the back. *How in the hell am I supposed to concentrate?* The majority of the students were from out of town, so they were staying at the hotel. I have to admit that I was a little envious, but I was also grateful to spend time my kids.

Class registration was at a table set up outside of the entry way. We were given a set of class materials, and name badges, and then we were asked to go in and take a seat. It was a small class, maybe twenty-five people. The chairs were set up facing the only wall that didn't have windows. The ocean was to our left, the patio was behind us, and the entrance from the hotel was to our right. I was so excited to be there. Because I was still struggling to understand the differences between a medium and a psychic, I was hoping to get an answer before the weekend was over.

One of Doreen's assistants came in, introduced herself, and went over housekeeping. After she was done, we knew where the bathrooms were, when breaks would occur, and where we could find restaurants and shops within walking distance of the hotel. And then it was time to get started. *Yay!*

When Doreen came in, everyone started applauding. Obviously, I was not her only fan. She began with an introduction for that one person in the room who didn't know who she was.

From the very beginning, Doreen encouraged us to believe in our abilities, to know that we were not there by accident, and to know that we were not alone. She followed this idea with an overview of the archangels (Michael, Raphael, Uriel, Gabriel, etc.) and the ascended masters (Jesus, Buddha, Quan Yin, etc.) she works with, and then she spoke about the fairy realm. It was fascinating to hear her speak. I thought I was crazy for believing that these realms existed, but there I was in class, listening to a beautiful woman who looked like my Barbie doll from childhood, and she was talking about these realms with complete sincerity. *Maybe I'm not crazy after all*, I thought. *And if I am, I have a whole bunch of people to keep me company.* I love staying positive.

Before we began our first exercise, she walked us through a meditation to relax our minds and prepare us to talk with spirits. I could have fallen asleep while sitting up in my chair and listening to Doreen's voice lead us through the opening of the chakra system, with emphasis on the third eye and crown. There was also a request sent out to all of our loved ones in spirit to come forth with any messages for us.

During our first exercise, I paired up with a gentleman named George. He was tall, attractive, and dressed like he could have stepped off the pages of a fashion magazine. Even his socks were perfect.

"Let's get comfortable sitting face-to-face with our partners," Doreen began. Some people stayed sitting in their chairs, some moved their chairs along the wall and sat on the carpeted floor. "Decide who will read first and who will receive."

I looked at George. "I'm completely new to this. Maybe you should go first." He smiled, nodded in agreement, and closed his eyes in meditation. I closed mine too. And then I heard his strong voice, so I opened my eyes to listen, watch, and learn. "I have two grandmothers here with me; do you have two grandmothers in spirit?"

"Yes," I replied.

"They are both strong women—different, very different—but strong."

"Yes," I replied again.

"They want you to know that they support you; they are aware of the difficulties you have been going through. They are proud of you, Rena, not disappointed. Know this. They are with you if you need their assistance; all you have to do is talk out loud or ask them to visit you in your dreams."

"Thank you." I whispered.

As George continued, I cried. It wasn't loud weeping but rather the quiet, please-don't-look-at-me kind of crying. I knew what George was talking about: my divorce, my children living in another state with their father, attending this crazy class, all of it. I broke the mold. I was neither good nor bad, but I was different from the women in my family before me.

George opened his eyes for the first time when Doreen instructed the readers to bring the reading to a close. When he saw I was cleaning up my mascara, he leaned forward and gave me a big hug. Then it was my turn to give a reading. *Oh dear God, please help me.* I called in my guardian angels and spirit guides. *Please help me relax, connect to George, and hear the messages that I receive clearly.*

"Readers, are you ready? Take a few deep breaths. Come on—don't be nervous; there is nothing to be nervous about. Just share the information you receive. Remember: there is no such thing as getting nothing," Doreen explained. "When you feel like you are ready, begin."

Like George taught me, I sat with my eyes closed, trying my hardest to stop talking to myself long enough to hear any messages. And then, all of sudden, I saw a picture of a man, a good-looking guy who was dressed like George. But then I felt my brother, Peter. *Huh? What does that mean? Is his name Pete or Peter?* Just as I was asking that question to myself, I realized that it *felt* like Peter. I opened my eyes, looked at George and said, "I see a man in spirit, a handsome man who dresses well. He reminds me of you." George nodded up and down.

"You were very close?" I asked. He nodded again. "He was your partner?" I asked. George's eyes were wide open.

"Yes," he said, and his eyes began to water.

"I am so sorry, George. He misses you very much, but he is worried about you. He wants you to move on; it's okay to move forward. He understands." We were both crying.

A few moments later, Doreen asked us to bring our readings to a close. I was relieved. It was all a little weird, like I was translating for spirit. I took visions and feelings and turned them into words. *Bizarre* ...

After a quick break, Doreen went over the positioning of deceased loved ones around the receiver. Basically, when you see spirits behind the left shoulder of the receiver, they are maternal grandparents. If they are farther out on the left, at arm's length, they are other maternal relatives, such as uncles, aunts, cousins, siblings, and even friends. If you see a spirit behind the right shoulder of the receiver they are paternal grandparents. If they are farther out on the right, at arm's length, they are other paternal relatives. The mother and father appear a bit higher around the side of the receiver's head.

This was all really interesting, but it was a lot of information to remember. Plus, I was not very good at remembering things when I was nervous. So instead, I made a bunch of notes on the handout and decided to stick it under my chair and go with my gut or whatever my clairvoyance showed me. Call me a cheater, but this is still how I give readings today.

It was time for the next exercise. We selected a new partner. Mine was Jim, who happened to be friends with George. He knew I was a nervous novice, which took a little of the edge off. Jim was a working medium; he knew his stuff inside and out. He was there for the practice and the certification.

I came to find out that there were a lot of professional mediums in class that day. My understanding is that certifications in this business are no different than in the regular business world: they are a gold star on your résumé, especially from a world-renowned instructor such a Doreen Virtue.

We decided to sit on the floor instead of the chairs this time. The new position was actually really comfortable. I asked Jim to go first, which he did.

Doreen began the exercise. "Okay, let's quiet down and prepare for our reading. Everyone take a few deep breaths. Just relax and focus on your breath as you clear your mind. When you are ready, you can begin."

Jim and I sat there with our eyes closed. As soon as Jim began talking, I opened my eyes. He started with a message from my grandmothers. It was very similar to George's, but then the focus shifted quickly to a new spirit, my brother, Peter. *Yay!*

"I see a young man, maybe in his late twenties. I believe he may be your brother," he said.

"Yes," I replied.

Jim went on to describe my brother: an attractive man who loved music, dancing, great food, and cooking. I knew it was him. But I wasn't sad, because I knew he was around me often. I was really relieved to know I wasn't making it up. Like my grandmothers, he wanted me to know he supported my decisions and was proud of me either way. But he loved Kurt too, so he reminded me to be nice. *What? I'm always nice. Pick a side already.*

And then it was my turn. I was already intimidated knowing that Jim was a professional. "Readers, take a few deep breaths, and begin when you feel ready," Doreen said. Surprisingly, her calming voice didn't help.

Jim and I sat there with our eyes closed. I waited and waited, and then I waited some more. *Oh my God … I've got nothing!* I was sure Jim had peeked out of one eye, wondering whether I was still there. I could hear the voices of the other students running a mile a minute around me, each describing deceased loved ones, their hobbies, their favorite foods. I could also hear my heart pounding in my chest. I sat there stiff and mute.

I was on the verge of hyperventilation and tears when I heard Jim's voice, "Rena, open your eyes. Just relax and take a deep breath. Remember, there is no such thing as getting nothing. We always get something. Sometimes we just need to start talking. Tell me anything that pops into your head. Let's get this started." I nodded, took a deep breath, closed my eyes, and then realized I could smell cookies.

I opened my eyes and said, "Cookies. I smell cookies!" Jim shot me a huge smile. As I was looking at him, I saw a woman appear from the waist up. "I see an older woman, she feels like a grandmother. She is a full-figured woman, she has her hair up in a bun or twist, and she is wearing a full apron. Is this your grandmother?" I asked.

"Yes," Jim replied.

"She is holding a baking sheet between her hands," I said, but then it quickly turned to a muffin tin. "Wait, it is a muffin tin. It looks like blueberry muffins. She is holding it right under my nose as if telling me to take one." Jim started laughing.

"Yes, that is correct. My grandmother loved to bake. Her favorite was blueberry muffins, and she would insist that you take one when you came to visit."

I was hooked. It was tiring, but I was hooked. How did I do that? How could I hear, see, smell, and feel these spirits? It was exciting but exhausting.

When we got up to take a break for lunch, I gave Jim a gigantic hug for helping me through the reading. It would have been an enormous train wreck, and I would have lost all self-confidence if he'd decided to be a pompous ass, but he hadn't. Instead, he had guided me through the process gently. He may have been worried I was going to run.

After lunch, we continued with more exercises. In between,

Doreen spent some time talking about the business side of mediumship, how to get the most out of a reading, ethics when giving a reading, and protection for both the reader and the receiver. *Protection from what?* I wondered. And then she went on to explain that the class was a certificate program. But in order to receive a certificate, we had to demonstrate our mediumship skills by standing up in front of the class and giving a blind reading.

Blind meant that the person just stood up there until a message came through, and then he or she shared it with the group in hopes that someone in the room could validate the information provided. This is called evidential mediumship. I was starting to faint just thinking about it.

Throughout the exercises and breaks that day, I met a young woman named Erica. Erica was a professional medium who was in the process of moving her business to the next level. She was well versed in the work of Doreen and many other well-known mediums. She had a very calm, nurturing personality that offset my high-strung, nervous self perfectly. Like Doreen, Erica worked with the angelic realm when she gave readings.

During one of the breaks, she gave me a gift called The Angels of Atlantis Chart that she developed. It was a laminated sheet that contained a large wheel split into thirteen sections that aligned with each of the archangels. On the back was a description of each one that included the associated color, essential oil, crystal, and affirmation.

To use the chart, you held the palm of your hand over the middle of the wheel, closed your eyes, asked your guides to be with you, and moved your hand clockwise until you felt an energy change, hot spot, or pull to one area. When you did, you lowered your middle finger onto the chart to get the number of the archangel. And then you used the back of the chart to identify the archangel and the associated details. *Genius! It's so simple. This is the greatest little divination tool ever!*

There were many times in the group exercises when I didn't speak up; instead, I whispered what I was getting to Erica to see whether she was picking up the same thing. After I did this a few times, she encouraged me to speak up. Not just for my own self-confidence but to keep the information flowing. It was a common challenge, and it was something that Doreen hounded us about over the weekend. "Don't be your own roadblock," she said. "Let the information that you are receiving out so that more information will come through."

Holding back the information you receive is like creating a dam. It blocks the information flow within you as it pounds away in your mind repeating itself over and over again. I have done this enough times over the last ten years to tell you it is true. Once you get the courage to open your mouth, the information begins to flow more rapidly. At times, it is difficult to process it quickly enough to translate it into words for the recipient. Because I was new, my translation time was long.

This was a challenge when sitting in a circle because, just when I started gathering information in my head, one of the other impatient students chimed in and piggybacked off of me. This is not as common in a development circle in the real world, but in a classroom where students are trying to impress the instructor, you may run into it a lot. I have.

Another common challenge is that even professional mediums can have brain freeze. This is when you present accurate information, but the receiver denies knowing who you are talking about, because, for whatever reason, he or she doesn't remember the person you are referring to at that moment. Let me give you a common example:

> **Me**: "I am getting a Bob or Robert, maybe Bobby. He feels like an uncle vibration. I can also taste cigarette smoke, so he was a smoker."
> **Jane**: "No, I don't recognize the name."
> **Me**: "He is showing me ice cream cones, strawberry."
> **Jane**: "No, sorry, I don't know anyone by that name."

Me: "Are you sure? He smoked. It feels like he may have died from cancer."

Jane: "No, he must be for someone else in the room."

Me: "No, he feels connected to you. I feel burning in my lungs it may have been lung cancer that he died from. He keeps showing me strawberry ice cream cones."

Jane: "Um, no, I really don't think he is for me," she says as she looks around the room.

Me: "Are you sure? Did your mom have a brother who passed away?"

Jane: "Oh! Wait! Yes, she did! He was my favorite uncle, Bob. His real name is Robert. He used to take me to get strawberry ice cream cones every Sunday after church. He died of lung cancer when I was twelve from smoking too much."

Yes, this really happens! And yes, it is really frustrating. You want to get up and slap the living daylights out of the person for being so thick, but you can't, because that wouldn't be professional.

When our class ended for the day, Doreen reminded us about the mediumship demonstration scheduled the next day for those interested in being certified. It was scheduled during the last half of class. Everyone was excited, even me.

"I want everyone to have fun with it. Please don't put a bunch of pressure on yourselves. Get some rest this evening so you are ready to go in the morning. Remember to try to stay away from excess amounts of caffeine and alcohol," she said as we were packing up for the day. Those last few words caused a look of pain on more than one face. I guess I wasn't the only one heading straight for the bar.

We were also encouraged to wear something new for the demonstration to give us a little boost. Our class materials contained a list of specialty shops within walking distance that sold the kind of flowing gowns that Doreen wore. I didn't know whether I could pull one off, but I wanted to try.

Erica and I went with a small group of women to see what we could find. I think Erica bought a scarf. I bought a hot pink shawl that was decorated with hot pink sequins. Because it was a wide weave, I could wear it over a black top with jeans. Plus, it was practically free compared to the flowing gown that I really wanted.

Sunday morning was all a buzz. We moved though our exercises in anticipation of the afternoon demonstration. Some women wore their new purchases from the day before. Mine was safely hidden away in my tote bag. After all, the demonstration was optional, and I could change my mind at any moment.

There was a large portion of time spent discussing self-promotion. This included brochures, seminars, and press kits for TV and radio. It was a great opportunity for questions that many of the students took advantage of. Because it was my first rodeo, however, I just sat back, took a few notes, and relaxed before the big show.

During break, everyone was asked to leave the room so that they could set things up. So off we went to change our clothes and touch up our make-up. I took my new shawl out and put it over my black knit top.

The doors opened and we were invited to go back in. Our chairs were set up in a half circle facing the only wall in the room. There were three chairs facing us for Doreen and her assistants. The energy in the room was high as everyone found a seat. I was ready to fake an illness. Stomach flu? Diarrhea? I could totally pull that off. But I stayed, sitting next to Erica, my rock. She smiled, squeezed my hand, and said, "Rena, breathe."

There is a term in the industry, *sitting for names,* that refers to the time when a medium is preparing to go in front of a group of people. The medium sits, quiets his or her mind, and listens for names that pop up. Once he or she gets a name, he or she uses it like grabbing onto the end of a piece of string and pulling gently until it begins to unravel. After that the information begins flowing.

Another term, *strolling for names,* entails the same process, except that the medium walks around on stage or in front of a group, listening for a name to come up. Strolling for names was my plan unless I heard one that wasn't used by one of the other students before it was my turn.

As the demonstration began, there was a group of students who volunteered to go first. They all appeared to be strolling for names as they walked around the room in front of us. It was brutal to watch—like eight slow-motion, head-on collisions in a row. Doreen and her assistants guided them along. They acted as our safety nets; they weren't going to let us crash and burn, but we had to work for it. In other words, we couldn't just stand there and claim to get nothing.

Like many of the classes I have taken that consisted of mainly women, we had a small pocket of personalities in the class. Like in the movies, these women were attractive and self-confident enough for all of us. I wanted to hate them, but they were too nice.

We all had great expectations for them, but sadly, it wasn't meant to be. They struggled through their demonstration like the rest of us. In their defense, there was a lot of brain freeze going on. In one case, I honestly wondered whether the receiver knew who the reader was talking about but intentionally made her sweat up there. Even Doreen gave the receiver a look.

The more I saw that group of women struggle, the more I wanted to run for the door. But Erica wouldn't let me. That woman could read my thoughts! We both knew I would regret it if I didn't try. "Rena, it's your turn," she said. I must have zoned out for a few seconds, because I didn't hear Doreen say my name. I looked at Erica, trying to find my confidence, and then I stood up and walked slowly to the middle of the room.

"Just relax, Rena, you can do this," Doreen said with an encouraging smile. I stood there, but I didn't feel or hear a thing, so I walked around the room, beginning at the far side from where I was sitting and worked my way back. I was nervous but holding it together.

Suddenly, I began to feel a pull to the middle of the room, so I followed it, which left me standing directly in front of the group of confident women. I started to feel a woman coming through. I looked up and they were all smiling back at me with honest encouragement. I took a step forward, but before I could speak, I got "vibed." This is what I call it when the energy shifts and feels painful. I started trembling, and then my stomach started hurting, so I immediately pulled back. The energy radiated from my solar plexus out to my fingertips. *What just happened?* I just stood there trying to process it when I heard Doreen say, "Rena, are you okay?"

"Yeah, I just got vibed over here. I don't know what happened," I said as I turned around. And then she said something I didn't expect: "Yes, we felt it too. Let's talk about it afterward. Keep walking around."

So I did. And when I heard the name Maria pop into my head, I looked to my right and heard it again. It was sharper the second time, and there was an accent to it. *Italian?* The woman speaking to me was rolling the <u>R</u> in her name. I then locked eyes with a woman sitting at the very end of the row and knew it was her. I walked over and said, "Do you have a grandmother in spirit named Maria?"

"Yes!" she said and flashed a beautiful smile.

"She is showing me flowers in a large flower box with heavy borders. Is this hers?" I asked.

"Yes."

"She said you look like her, that people tell you that you remind them of her. Is that correct?"

"Yes."

"She wants you to know that she is still with you. Do you smell flowers around the house at random times?"

"Yes! I thought it was just me!"

I laughed and said, "No, it is your grandmother letting you know that she is with you." The reading went on. I want to say it included validation about her decision to go to college or not.

When I finished, I gave Erica a hug and sat down. She was

proud of me, and I was proud of myself. I barely remember the students who went after me, because I was so deep into my own thoughts.

When everyone was done, there was a question and answer session. I shared what I experienced when I got vibed. It turned out that Doreen and her assistants felt the energy shift where they were sitting too. Apparently, that activity is common when a spirit does not want you to be the medium that delivers the message to a loved one. Basically, I got the get-the-hell-away vibe.

I went home to Kurt and the kids that evening stoned on my own self-confidence. My arm hurt from patting myself on the back so much during the drive home. Even the traffic couldn't kill my buzz. I stood up in the living room giving them a play-by-play account of the whole event while still wearing my hot pink poncho. I got hugs and high fives. They were proud of their Momster, and I was proud I didn't fake diarrhea.

I still have my pink poncho. I pull it out of the closet every now and then and put it on. It reminds me to stand tall, trust what I get, and remember that there is no such thing as getting nothing.

What I Learned in Class

- Mediumship is real—and apparently I am one.
- The difference between a psychic and a medium is that a medium communicates with entities in the spirit world (past loved ones, both human and pets, spirit guides, angels, etc.) and may share messages from them with those in the physical world. A psychic shares information obtained using the *Clair Senses,* chakras, auras, telepathy, etc. Both are equally awesome.
- To have faith in our guides; they won't let us down.
- Dead people have a lot to say.

Six Sensory Professional Practitioner Level 1 with Sonia Choquette

It was March of 2005, and I was getting ready to take Sonia's Six Sensory class, which was held in Itasca, Illinois, at the Eaglewood Resort. My flight got in late, so I scheduled an executive car service to drive me from the airport to the hotel. The service was recommended in an e-mail sent to us prior to class, so I didn't anticipate any problems. Nevertheless, I was feeling sick that week, so the trip was already starting off a little bumpy. The only option was to take some over-the-counter meds and move on.

I was living in Tustin, California, around the corner from Kurt. I moved there the first week in January, leaving my three-bedroom home with a two-car garage behind for a two-bedroom apartment that was twice the price each month than my mortgage had been. To make things worse, the large financial institution that I worked for had just acquired another bank. This meant another reorganization that led my senior leader to move me into an individual contributor role under a woman I had never met. But it gave me the opportunity to move to California. Since I was a regional manager, I had to be on-site, but not any longer. Life was definitely a challenge. I was incredibly happy to be with my kids again, but I felt like everything else in my life had died.

Kurt and the kids dropped me off at the airport, wishing me well and making me promise to call when I landed and made it to the resort. My flight arrived on time, but my driver didn't. Because it was after eleven o'clock at night, I was more than a little nervous. I called the number I was given for a direct connection to my driver. When he answered the phone, I knew he had been asleep. "Hi, this is Rena, your 10:30 p.m. appointment. I'm here waiting at baggage claim. Are you close?" I knew he wasn't.

"Um, what? Who is this again?" I repeated myself and added, "Were you asleep?" I could hear him shuffling through some paperwork.

"I'm sorry," he explained, "I must have overslept. Unfortunately, I'm not going to make it. You will have to take a taxi." *WHAT?*

"Are you serious? I made these reservations a month ago. The whole reason I booked the appointment with you in the first place is because you were recommend by the instructor," I said while grinding my teeth. Silence.

"I don't know what to tell you. Because of the distance, it will take too long for me to get ready and get there," he said.

ARUUUGH!

After some more heated debate, I hung up and went outside for a taxi. It was almost midnight. The whole taxi thing felt sketchy, but I had no choice. *Dear God, please don't let my driver be an axe murderer. Please let me arrive in one piece and not be found dead along the side of some random road. Thank you. Amen.*

I placed my suitcase in the trunk, because apparently in Chicago the taxi drivers don't have strong enough arms. After that, I got into the back seat and provided the driver with the name and address of the resort. He had never heard of it and had no idea where it was. *Of course he has never heard of it. The flu was a sign; I should have stayed home.*

We drove in circles for over an hour, stopping several times so he could call dispatch and get new directions. It was so dark outside that I couldn't see a thing. It was cold, I was starving, and panic was setting in. Finally, after the millionth call to dispatch, we arrived.

Fortunately, I managed to get a small pizza from the bar area.

I practically inhaled the food, and then I dropped on the bed and passed out.

The next morning, I had breakfast in my room before heading down to the conference area for registration. Sonia's assistant greeted us and checked our names off the list. There were no handouts or class materials of any kind—not even a free pen. *Interesting,* I thought. I was expecting more given the price of the class, but I shrugged it off because it was only my second one. Besides, I brought my own paper, pen, post-its, and highlighters.

The class was such a contrast to the mediumship program in sunny California. The resort was nice, but the views were not. It was still winter, and everything was dead, cloudy, and gray outside. The large, heavy curtains in the room were partly drawn. My guess is that it was to keep our focus on class, not the dark and eerie landscape outside. It was a large room with a stage that was raised up about a foot and a half. The chairs were set up in two main sections, and an aisle ran down the middle. There were at least seventy-five students, certainly more. I took an aisle seat in the back row with a great view.

There was a stool and a microphone on the left side of the stage for Mark Stanton Welch, who played the guitar. Mark looked like the actor Javier Bardem. There was also a tall chair and a second microphone for Sonia on the other side.

Mark had gone up on stage while we were checking in. He was all smiles and said, "Good morning!" to some of the students along the way. He then tuned his guitar and began playing music for us while we settled in. It was wonderful. But it had a familiar feeling that I couldn't place.

Sonia came in shortly afterward. She said a few words to her assistant before proceeding toward the stage. From what I saw, she didn't make eye contact with anyone. In fact, she looked angry. No smile, no joy, nothing. She walked over to Mark, he smiled, she nodded, and then she took the mic from the stand and looked around the room. And that's when it hit me: it felt like church—Catholic church to be exact! There was a quiet vibe. It was as if we were all in trouble and getting ready to repent for our sins. *Oh no! What the hell did I get myself into?*

Sonia began with a short introduction of herself and Mark. She provided some background about how long they had been working together. And then she talked about why we were probably there: a calling, a need, psychic awareness opening up, etc. Finally, she gave us an overview of what to expect over the next several days. She also introduced her guides and the roles that they would play during readings and in her life in general. This is when the discussion turned to the ego.

"In order to hear your guides, you will need to learn how to put your ego aside," Sonia explained. *Hmm, exactly how do we do that?* There was a lot of discussion about our egos over those three days. Apparently, just by glancing at people, someone could tell that egos were present, not higher selves. The ego was bad and full of self-defense mechanisms. Basically, an all-around pompous ass.

We were barely moving into the third hour of class when a "needy one" reared its ugly head. "Needy ones" are people who take every opportunity to make the class about them. They talk about their divorces, separations, losses of a pet, job struggles, etc. By the time you leave, you could write their biographies.

What I have figured out over the years is that they are not there to learn. What they really want is a reading and group therapy. In this case, it was a woman, and she was bitter. Right away, she began asking questions about her guides and why they don't talk to her regardless of how hard she tries. *Maybe because you have anger issues and are stuck in your ego!* I thought. Sonia spent a good amount of time with her. She explained the process she could use to connect to her guides while we all listened impatiently for the drama to end. When it did, the needy one was in tears, and we all applauded her breakthrough. It was not what I wanted to pay for with my very large tuition fee, but I reminded myself that it was only the first day.

There was also a lot of singing while Mark played the guitar.

This activity was designed to get us out of our egos. Apparently, they don't like the noise. I was very uncomfortable because I can't sing. At all. So being asked to do so was like stabbing myself in the leg with a dull butter knife. Eventually, I got past my fears though, and I began to sing along. I felt completely ridiculous, like I was standing in church—but what the hell. I was already there, so why not? I was surprised to find that it actually worked: I relaxed.

We finally moved on to some exercises to help us tune into our higher selves and spirit guides. Mark played the guitar in the background as we were guided through a meditation. When the music stopped, we heard Sonia's voice: "Everyone, grab a partner and sit facing each other." We did as we were told, moving chairs here and there around the room, leaving plenty of space for privacy. "Decide who is going to read first." We did. "Relax. Remember: you are not here to prove anything to anyone. That is your ego. You are here to learn to be of service, to be a channel for the information that you receive from your guides and their loved ones in spirit." *Great, now I'm totally in my ego.* "When the readers are ready, begin."

Because I was the reader, I sat there with my eyes closed, took a few deep breaths, and waited. I was so nervous that my hands were shaking. And then the information began to flow slowly. I kept my eyes closed and shared everything with the young woman sitting across from me.

"I see backpacking in the mountains, funky clothes (like the seventies), and a pink Volkswagen Beetle," I said. "I also see young man, maybe a boyfriend. It feels like he could be a boyfriend if you wanted to take that friendship to the next level. You spend time with him camping." Most of the reading revolved around this possible relationship. I felt like she was on the fence, but I didn't know why.

By keeping my eyes closed, I had no immediate validation to alter what I was receiving; instead, I had to trust what I received.

When the reading came to an end, we were given the opportunity to validate the information with the receiver. The woman explained that she drove a pink Volkswagen Beetle. The guy that I saw her with was her best friend, whom she had recently began having intimate feelings for. She was worried that, if he didn't feel the same way, bringing it up would ruin the friendship.

We did this type of exercise several times with different partners. It was lot of fun and got me out of my ego that appeared every time we had to sing.

During one of the evenings, we were invited to attend a class taught by Mark. We were told to wear comfortable clothes and shoes. If we didn't have sneakers, we were encouraged to wear a pair of socks. We met in the same conference room, but the chairs were moved against the walls. Mark played the guitar while we danced, sang, and chanted through different exercises.

In one, we stood in two giant circles, one within the other facing each other. We had to sing different affirmations to each other, and then the middle circle turned to the right, so that we switched partners. We then sung another affirmation. It was crazy. To date, I sang more in that long weekend then I sang in the rest of my life combined.

Our last exercise of the evening was a little different. There was a young man named Chris, and he was very ill. I don't know what his illness was—I never asked—but he was tall and thin, had pale skin, and had just a few tufts of hair left on his head.

"Okay, everyone, let's form a large circle," Mark said. We immediately followed his instructions. "Chris, please go into the middle of the circle, lie down on your back, and relax." Chris smiled and moved into the middle of the circle as Mark continued. "We are going to chant the words that I will give you in just a minute. All the while, I will play the guitar. I want you to relax into the music as you open up your heart and channel love and healing through yourselves and into Chris." We all nodded in agreement. I could tell that everyone was onboard and ready to get started. And then Mark shared the words that we would say over and over again as he led the rhythm and pace with his guitar. "I will be chanting along with you. Please continue until I stop playing. Ready to get started? " YEAH! "Okay, everyone hold hands." And that's what we did.

It started slowly at first as we all got the hang of it, and then the pace increased a little more. Chris looked lovely lying on the floor; he seemed relaxed, like he could float away at any moment. And then the chants became more forceful and intense as the rhythm took us forward. People were swaying side to side, but our hands remained locked together. And then the strangest thing happened: I started to feel light-headed, like I was going to faint. After that, I was overcome with emotion. Tears started flowing down my cheeks, but my lips kept moving. And then, as if in a dream, I began reaching out to Chris. I let go of the hands I was holding, knelt down on my hands and knees, and crawled over to him. I found myself behind the top of his head, sitting with my feet underneath me. I placed both my hands on his head with the base of my hands at the crown, and the tips of my fingers toward his eyes. I felt a rush of energy and emotion run through me as tears continued to fall down my face.

I'm not sure how long I was there. At some point, the chanting ended and a few of my classmates came over to help Chris and me up. I felt exhausted but wide awake. I had no mascara left, but I was in good shape otherwise. As we left the room that night, Chris and I gave each other a huge hug.

Later, I was told that Chris had experienced a surge of heat that flowed from his head through his body during the time my hands were on him. He also fell into a semi-meditative state, like I did, with no sense of time. That was really interesting to hear.

I don't know what happened that evening. I can share the story, but I can't offer any scientific explanation. Maybe it was the power of group prayer mixed with music, chanting, and pure love with no strings attached. All I know is that I was called to him … and I answered.

Our last day was like the ones before it. We sang, learned the highs and lows of the business from both Sonia and Mark, had a good question-and-answer session, and gave each other readings. I am happy to say that mine ended on a high note.

I think Jill was in her early thirties, with dark blonde hair and a tired look about her. We were practicing psychometry, so Jill handed me a large pearl necklace.

Psychometry entails reading an object by touching or holding it. It works the same way as giving a reading for a person, but your focus stays on the object in your hand. After you hold the object, you provide the impressions, sights, smells, and feelings that you get to the receiver. I love psychometry.

As I held the necklace, I felt a grandmother and mother presence around us. I could actually feel her mother breathing down my neck. Her mother's personality was strong and intense, a force to be reckoned with. My head began pounding from her energy. I started to rub my forehead, which concerned Jill a bit.

"I can see a large, beautiful house with a gravel road leading up to the driveway. I see cocktails, martinis, and you dancing in a little, yellow dress." Jill's eyes widened, "Yes, that is correct."

"I feel a mother and a grandmother here with us."

"Yes, they are both in spirit."

"Your mother wants you to know that it is okay to be yourself. She is very proud of you and is very sorry for not telling you that when you were growing up. You are perfect the way you are. If you want to wear her pearls with a cardigan sweater, jeans, and tennis shoes, do it! You are not your mother's daughter, you are better!"

Jill's eyes opened up and looked like they were going to pop out of her head and into my hands. Tears started welling up in her eyes, and I could see the relief on her face as the weight lifted off her body. The music started playing, and she jumped up and started dancing with her hands in the air saying, "I am not my mother's daughter! I am not my mother's daughter!" And then she gave me a huge hug and said, "Thank you, Rena!" As she continued to dance around the room with the rest of us crazies.

It took a while before I got rid of the headache from Jill's mom, but seeing Jill jumping around visibly happier made it worth every pounding second.

What I Learned in Class

- Just go with it. Even if you are asked to sing, great things can and will happen.
- The difference between psychic and mediumship readings from experience.
- Whining about your life in class can get you a free reading with the instructor, but it will piss off your classmates.
- Sonia was spot-on about the ego thing. I still use that theory today.
- Mark's music rocks! I bought several of his CDs.

Learn to Awaken Your Psychic Strengths with John Holland

Two months later, I attended a one-day class with John Holland at the Learning Light Foundation in Anaheim, California. The Learning Light is a two-story church that was converted into a learning center in 1962.

It was a beautiful, clear, sunny day that morning as I drove to class. It was held in the conference room upstairs that had stained glass windows. Someone opened them, and let in a cool breeze. It was a smaller class, maybe twenty-five or thirty people. There were two sets of rows facing the front of the room and a small aisle running down the middle. In the front of the class, there was a small table set up for John. There was also an easel with paper and markers.

It was a casual environment. All the students seemed really relaxed as we picked our seats and got settled in. Because the back rows were already taken, I sat in the front row. I felt exposed, but I managed to hold it together.

John entered the room with a cup in his hand. "Good morning, everyone!" He said, as he made his way to the front of the room where he began his introduction. I found it really funny because of his great sense of humor and Boston accent. I couldn't stop listening if I wanted to. When he was finished, he opened the floor for questions before we moved on.

Because the class was about how to access our psychic strengths, we were given an overview of how to access the information psychically using our *Clair Senses,* the seven main chakra energy centers, and our auras.

The word *chakra* is a Sanskrit term that means wheel of light. They are described as a type of revolving door or portal between our bodies, minds, and souls. They are points of connection that allow energy to flow from one person to another, and they connect us to the multidimensional universe. Each of the seven chakras serves a different purpose.

> **First chakra** (also known as base or root): Red, located at the hip/genital area, linked to basic survival instincts.
> **Second chakra**: Orange, located at the abdomen, linked to creativity.
> **Third chakra**: Yellow, located at the solar plexus, linked to personal power.
> **Forth chakra**: Green, located at the heart, linked to love and healing.
> **Fifth chakra**: Blue, located at the throat, linked to communication and expression.
> **Sixth chakra** (third eye): Indigo, located in the middle of the forehead, linked to insight and visions.
> **Seventh chakra**: White, located at the crown of the head, linked to divine awareness and higher knowing.

The aura is an energy field that resembles a band of light and surrounds all living things (people, plants, animals, etc.). It has six main auric layers, each a different color. Similar to the chakras, each auric layer is associated with a different purpose. The aura can provide information regarding physical health.

John dimmed the lights and stood in front of the wall at the front of the room to give a demonstration of what an aura looks like. "Focus on the area above my head," he said. "Relax your eyes.

You will begin to see a golden or yellow light around my head and shoulder area."

I could see the yellow-white light all around him, but I couldn't see any other colors. He explained to the class that only seeing golden or yellow light was common, but it could be improved with practice.

After the demonstration, we took a quick break before moving into the first psychic development exercise. John brought a set of large pictures with him to class. He held one up so that only one side of the room could see it. "Take a good look at the picture. Don't say anything out loud. If you need to make a few notes about what you see, write them down," he explained. And then he put the picture down and said, "I want you to send the image that you saw in the picture to the other half of the room." We all started to chuckle as we listened to John's instructions. And then he turned to us on the opposite side of the room and said, "I want you guys to relax, take a deep breath, close your eyes if you want to, and write down any images you receive. Got it?" We all nodded our heads. "Okay, let's get started!"

The opposite side of the room was staring at us like we were barbequed steak and they were rabid dogs. It was kind of funny. I wrote down the images I received, and then I put my pen down. I received water, sand, palm trees, and several long, thin boats. When our side was ready, John asked us to share what we received with the other side of the class. We all took turns.

"What do you guys think, did they do well?" he asked the group who saw the photo. "Yeah!" they replied in unison, and then he held it up for us to see.

It was a picture of a beach with several palm trees that were bent forward toward the ocean, with about five long, colorful, thin boats pulled ashore. *Whooohoo!*

Now it was our turn to send images to them. John held up a picture of a field of sunflowers. When he gave the go ahead, we began sending the image to the other side of the room while they wrote things down. After a few minutes, John asked them to share what they received.

"I kept seeing the picture by Monet called a *Bouquet of Sunflowers,*" one man said. *Wow, he nailed it.* The picture wasn't Monet, but he was correct. Another student said, "I kept getting baseball and sunflower seeds." *Ha! That was totally me!* I kept thinking about eating sunflower seeds at Travis's baseball games. He nailed it too. After John held up the picture for them to see, I told the man who kept seeing a baseball game that he wasn't crazy, it was me sending that image. The whole class got a good laugh out of it. The results were really impressive. The exercise was focused on teaching us how we receive information (see, hear, taste, smell, feel). It was very effective.

Toward the end of class, the coolest thing happened. We were sitting in our seats, John was standing up and looking down at something on one of the student's desks in the front row. Suddenly, when I looked over, I saw a full aura around him. I could see at least six layers of color. It looked like a rainbow flowing out from his entire body about a foot wide. I tried to make it go away by blinking, not fully believing what I was seeing, but it stayed around him until he walked back to the front of the class. It was brilliant. I couldn't wait to tell Kurt!

What I Learned in Class

- Auras exist.
- We can communicate telepathically.
- X-Men are real!

Experiencing the Spirit World with A.J. Barrera

In August, I took a one-day class with A.J. Barrera designed to unleash our psychic and mediumship abilities. It was held at The Enlightenment Books & Gifts store in Riverside, California. A.J. was a local medium. My daughter, Sydney, and I saw him for the first time during a demonstration at the Learning Light weeks before. He was incredibly accurate and had a light-hearted personality when he gave his readings.

On the day of his demonstration, Sydney and I were cut off by a woman in the parking lot. I said a few choice words and flipped her the bird from the safety of my truck that had tinted windows.

During the reading, my brother, Peter, came through. As we listened to A.J. speak, he started to transform, taking on my brother's mannerisms. It was incredible to watch. And then he said, "Your brother said that you look all professional and nice sitting there, but you're really not." Sydney and I started laughing, and he continued: "He told me that you were in an argument or something in the parking lot before you got here." And then we really started laughing because the woman was sitting a few rows up!

A.J. went on to tell my daughter to keep writing. At that time, she wanted to go college for journalism. And then he looked at me and said, "You too. He said both of you should keep writing." I had no idea what he meant. At that time, I was just getting into reading, not writing. And then came an even bigger surprise: "Are you famous? Are you a well-known figure in the public or something like that?" he asked.

"No," I said, a little shocked.

"Wow, that is weird. I saw lights around you. That is my sign for someone who is famous." Sydney and I just looked at each other. *A.J., if you are reading this book, I'm still waiting patiently dude!*

A.J. kicked off the class with introductions. It was a small bookstore, and there were only about twelve students. He provided each of us with a folder filled with class materials and a pen. I thought that was really generous considering the low price of the class tuition.

He went through an overview of the *Clair Senses,* chakras, and auras, and then we began the development exercises.

We gave each other readings in pairs and as a group. We used objects and pictures that A.J. brought, but the only reading I really remember is a group exercise we did using a photo. I don't remember what was in the photo, only that the information I received was a bougainvillea plant and a hanging, stained-glass wind chime. I was way off that day.

Still, I had a great time. I spent most of the day laughing with the owner of the shop, who was a fellow student. I also heard from Peter, I think. A young woman in her early twenties gave me a reading in a group exercise, and she picked up many of his traits and his cause of death, but not a message. Instead she got a mouth full of ectoplasm. Allegedly, it formed in her throat while she was trying to speak. We all watched, but she didn't do anything obvious like foam at the mouth. So after a few minutes of staring, we moved on to the next exercise.

What I Learned in Class

- Stay light-hearted and expect anything.
- Ectoplasm is real … kind of.

Angel Therapy Practitioner (ATP) Course with Doreen Virtue

In October, I attended Doreen Virtue's ATP certification course, held at the Surf & Sand Resort in Laguna Beach, California. By this time, I had been living in southern California for ten months. During that time the housing market and gas prices went insane—house prices doubled overnight, making it impossible for me to own one again. The silver lining to the gas prices in the four dollar range was that I could telecommute a few days per week. Eventually that led to working from home full-time. I turned into a stay-at-home working mom who never left her apartment. I became a hermit.

I decided early on that I wanted to stay at the hotel as a type of getaway for the duration of the class. I hoped that listening to the ocean waves at night would ease the mass depression taking over my day-to-day life. Besides, I was looking forward to hanging out with like-minded people while trying to find answers to my unraveled life. By this time, Doreen had several decks of oracle cards on the market, and I owned two of them. Kurt and the kids gave me Goddess Guidance on Valentine's Day, and I bought the other one, Healing with the Angels.

On the first day, I checked into my room before class registration. My room sat right above the sand, and the view took my breath away. Quickly, I unpacked and went over to the conference room.

Tables were set up outside the two sets of double doors for

registration. They were broken down by last name to speed up the process. Dozens of people were waiting in lines all around me.

"Hi, last name *Huisman* and first name *Rena*," I said to the woman on the other side of the table. She searched her binder of names, looked up, and said, "I'm sorry, can you please spell that for me?" I did. Once again, she checked her book. The confused look on her face said it all: I wasn't on the list.

"Give me a moment," she said in a sweet tone, "I will be right back." Immediately, she got up and walked over to a few women standing behind the tables overseeing everything. One of them came back to the table with her.

"We apologize, Rena, but your name is not on the list. By any chance did you print out a copy of the confirmation e-mail and bring it with you?" *YES I DID!* I opened my bag and handed it to them. They looked relieved.

With the confirmation in hand, they registered me and created my name badge. While this was happening, the woman behind the table explained that they had upgraded their system and somehow lost dozens of names. They knew their count was off, but they had no way of identifying the missing names. This is also why I never received any email correspondence leading up to the event.

When the paperwork was complete, the woman bent over in her chair and pulled something out of a box on the floor. She then set the stack down on the table in front of me. "There you go. Have fun!"

"This is for me?" I asked. My eyes were wide open.

"Yes, you'll need a deck of oracle cards for the class exercises. The books are for your enjoyment," she said and shot me a huge smile and a wink. "Thank you so much." I mumbled in confusion, as I picked up everything and walked toward the conference room. *Wow! I got a deck of oracle cards and two books for free!*

The conference room was light and bright with pop music playing in the background. The energy was high as I looked across the room. It was obvious that everyone was really happy to be there.

There were a dozen or more volunteers working at the three-day event. They were certified ATPs, and they were all professional psychics, mediums, and/or healers who volunteered to help the next group coming through. They answered questions, prepped the room for the different exercises, and shared their success stories throughout the weekend. They also provided sign-up sheets for a reading or healing for a small fee. It was a win-win situation for them. They were able to go through the course again for free as volunteers, grow their personal businesses in the evening by giving out business cards and offering readings, and add all that experience to their résumés. I looked up to them in awe.

There was no stage, but I saw large chairs and a couple of mics in the front of the room for Doreen and her assistant, Kelly. Kelly was a beautiful, tall, brunette woman who had a mind as sharp as Doreen's. They were like two tomboys hidden in beautiful princess gowns.

Kelly was in charge of keeping things on track and not allowing any of the students to take up too much time. The role was vital considering the fact that Doreen didn't give personal readings anymore. If people were there to air their personal problems for a group reading, it wasn't going to happen on Kelly's watch. She had a gentle way of shutting them down and moving things along. I also noticed some people legitimately starstruck by Doreen. They seemed a little creepy to me.

Because Doreen is a huge fan of hands-on learning, we gave each other readings numerous times with different partners using our new oracle cards. We experimented with one-, two-, and three-card spreads.

In a one-card spread, you focus on what the receiver needs to know at that point in time or a specific question. In a two-card spread, you focus on the present and the future. In a three-card spread, you focus on the past, present, and future.

As the reader, I shuffled my deck and let the receiver pull the cards and place them face down. And then I turned them over and began the reading. Some people used the cards literally; they read the words on the cards or in the booklet first. I preferred to tell them what I received intuitively before looking at what was written on the card or in the booklet. After all, the picture on the card or the words on the card might not be information I was receiving. This process shifts when I pull cards for myself though; in that case, I always read the message for each card in the booklet that came with the deck.

There were a few women who insisted that I was doing it wrong. According to them, I was supposed to read the description on the card and the message in the book, not pay attention to what I received intuitively. These were not smart women.

Doreen presented several guided meditations, but the one about money was a particularly eye-opening exercise for me. She explained, "There are many people who have preconceived ideas about money. This includes what can and cannot earn them a living. The term *starving artist* is a good example. Why do I have to be starving if I'm an artist?" We just stared at her. It was a good question; after all, I knew people who are very successful artists in many niches. "The answer is we don't," she said. "These may be things we heard growing up that are now programmed in our thoughts. This meditation is designed to help identify and remove any blocks you may have about money. Sound good?" We all nodded in agreement. "Okay, everyone spread out and get comfortable. Make sure that you have paper and a pen handy so you can journal what you receive."

Some students stayed in their chairs, others were lying down on the carpet. I decided to sit on the ground with my legs crossed in front of me. I made sure my paper and pen were within reach. We closed our eyes and relaxed as Doreen led us through the meditation while some nice background music accompanied her words on the CD player.

Moments later, she asked us to open our eyes and take out a

dollar bill or whatever we had with us. I grabbed a twenty from my wallet. "You are going to have a conversation with the money in your hand. Ask it about your relationship to it. Is it positive? Negative? Why?" she explained.

Hey, paper dude, how can I multiply you times a billion? I will admit I felt a bit foolish, but she was right. Many people are brought up believing that having a lot of money is bad, that it is the root of all evil, that anyone who has more than a fair share will suffer some unlucky consequence. For some reason, the guy who lives around the corner in the big house with a Porsche is a horrible person. He is probably an unfriendly ass who cheats on his wife because he has a lot of money.

I was brought up in a middle-class family, but money was tight. I was acutely aware of how much we didn't have at times, and yes, the wealthier families did appear to be a bunch of a-holes. Still, I knew that one day, *I* would live on the other side of those tracks in a big house with a Porsche. Who cared if they called me a horrible person? I could handle it. With that thought, I held out my twenty dollar bill and began to speak internally, *Hey, how is it going? I don't think you are bad at all. In fact, I would like to see a whole lot more of you and your bigger friends.* The weird thing is, while I was chatting away, information started entering my mind about times in my life when negative views of people with money surfaced.

My internal discussion was about my aspirations. I wanted more for myself and my family than I had growing up, but I felt bad about that. I thought that such an urge implied that I didn't have enough growing up, but that wasn't true. Sure, a built-in pool and a trampoline would have been nice (and yes, it sucked that our neighbors had them, not us). But we did fine without them. I didn't want to hurt my parents' feelings by wanting more. That was my break-through.

There was a good amount of singing and dancing to pop music in addition to the intuitive exercises. I distinctly remember being part of a conga line one afternoon. But the highlight of the weekend occurred during the last evening, when we were invited to an optional class held by Doreen's husband at the time, Steven Farmer. Steven is a shaman who works with animal spirit guides. At that time, I was vaguely familiar with his work.

We were told to wear comfortable clothes, so I dressed in my yoga pants and a jacket. I had a light dinner in my room earlier, so I was ready to embrace the shamanic class. When I got there I was greeted by a dozen other students dressed in sweats and yoga pants. There were also several ATP volunteers there to provide instructions once everyone arrived. As we were waiting, they advised us to use the restroom before we entered the conference room—once we were inside, we could not leave until the ceremony was over. *Did she say ceremony?*

The double doors to the conference room were locked, but we could hear them inside moving things around. Finally, one of the volunteers came outside and gave the other ATPs a nod. *Get on with it already! The freaking suspense is killing me!*

"Okay, let's get started. When the doors open, an ATP will be standing on each side of the entryway. Stop just before you cross over the threshold so they can smudge you with sage. This is to clear your energy field before you enter the room. Do you understand?" We all nodded. "The room will be dark when you enter, so it will take a few minutes for your eyes to adjust. An ATP will be on the other side to guide you to your place in the circle to take a seat. Please do not talk during this process. Are there any questions?" We all shook our heads. *We get an aura bath, get escorted to our seats, and have to refrain from talking. Got it.*

The ATP continued, "When everyone is inside, the doors will be closed and locked, and then the entryway will be smudged. When that is complete, Steven will begin the ceremony," Right about then, we heard a *click* as the doors opened. We fell into line as the process began.

Because I was near the middle of the line, I couldn't see much, just the outline of the ATPs inside stepping forward to escort the students to their seats.

When it was my turn, I stepped forward to receive the smudge. I tried not to laugh. Both ATPs held albacore shells in their hands that contained sage. They used a feather to move the smoke around me from head to toe and then back up again. I could tell the ATPs were trying not to laugh as well. And then my escort arrived and walked me over to my place in the circle. I sat down, nodded, and patted her arm gently to show my appreciation.

All the lights in the room were off, and the light from the outside was completely blocked out by heavy curtains. The only light in the room was a campfire in the middle of the circle. At first I thought it was real, thinking about all the fire code violations and wondering where the fire extinguishers were. But then I realized the flames were not real; they were crafted out of little lightbulbs buried underneath logs of wood set up strategically on a reflective surface.

By the time the last person entered the circle, it had grown into a spiral two people deep. I was grateful I was in the front row with plenty of time to relax amid the sounds of nature and drums playing in the background.

Finally, the doors were locked and smudged. It was time to begin. Steven handed out small drums and rattles to us. I got a rattle. I wondered if the woman behind me was jealous. He explained very briefly who he was and what a shaman did before we began.

"In this ceremony, we will work animal guides. We will invoke them through chanting while using the drums and the rattles," he said. Steven looked like the actor in the movie *Crocodile Dundee*. He appeared rugged, as if he spent a lot of time camping and hiking. It was easy to listen to whatever he said, and we were all mesmerized.

The sounds of nature faded as the sounds of native drums intensified. And then Steven began to chant. We followed along with our drums and rattles as instructed. The rhythm raised the vibration in the room quickly. Moments later, as if he were a conductor, he instructed us to place our instruments down gently.

After that, Steven began invoking the animal spirits that would serve as our protectors: the hawk and the eagle.

Steven was standing to my left, eyes looking up to the sky. His hands lifted slightly out in front of him as he said, "Mighty hawk, we ask that you watch over us tonight as we journey to the other side to meet our animal spirit guides. We ask that you keep us safe from any harm. Thank you for your service." We all sat quietly. He then closed his eyes and put his hands together while standing there silently.

Soon thereafter, he opened his eyes and lifted his arms up to begin invoking the eagle. Suddenly, I heard the loud sound of air moving by me and a piercing squawk. I jumped, looked around to see whether anyone else heard the noise, and saw that everyone else remained motionless. Everyone's eyes were still on Steven, but then it happened again: *swoosh, squawk!* By that point, Steven was finishing up the invocation for the eagle. I sat there, completely freaked out and looking at him with an expression that said, *Didn't you hear that?* He just continued.

At that moment, I looked straight up and saw that the ceiling was no longer there. I could see the sky perfectly when two gigantic birds flew in! *Oh. My. God.* They flew right over my head, one in front of the other, and then they looped back around. I felt like everything was moving in slow motion. Their wingspans were easily twelve feet across, and their bodies were the size of large German shepherds. I could feel the breeze created by their movement and thought, *Am I really the only one who sees them?* They were breathtaking. As the ceremony continued, they both remained perched on an invisible branch to my left, watching over us like two body guards.

We chanted, drummed, rattled, and danced our way through the ceremony until it was time to close down. Once again, Steven stood up, looked up to the sky with his arms out in front of him, and thanked the hawk and the eagle for their service. The moment Steven finished his sentence, they looked down at him, nodded, and flew away. This was one of my favorite experiences during my journey. To this day, I feel incredibly blessed to have been a part of that ceremony.

During the last day of class, we learned how to cut etheric cords. An etheric cord is like a string of energy that connects you to someone else, an energetic bond that looks like a cord or rope made of energy. The cords send and receive energy between chakras (heart to heart or heart to solar plexus). As a result of establishing an etheric cord, you can't stop thinking about the person to whom you are connected. In short, you feel like you can't move on from events surrounding that person, even when you go to sleep. Some people can see etheric cords. Others use their hands to detect the cords by gliding them a few inches above the person's head or body until they feel them.

There are many ways to cut cords. We learned to do so by asking for assistance from our guides—for example: "Dear spirit guides, please help me cut any etheric cords that are no longer serving my higher purpose. Please surround me with beautiful, white healing light to protect me from future attachments." You can also keep it simple by saying, "I cut all etheric cords that are no longer serving my higher purpose." This can be followed by moving your hand like a knife in front of your solar plexus and heart. I still use these exercises when I feel like I am being drained by someone else. I follow it by surrounding myself with a pink bubble of protection (think Glinda the Good Witch) filled and surrounded with beautiful, white light that comes straight from heaven (or moonlight or universal energy or whatever you wish).

One thing that surprised me that weekend was the number of professionals attending the class for the ATP certification. This was good and bad for the students attending the class to learn and practice. It was nice because advice was readily available, but it was bad because there was a chance of encountering a pompous ass who thought they already knew everything, and just wanted to get through the weekend with the least amount of effort. The good ones helped people through their readings, including offering moral support and encouragement. The bad ones looked bored and made others feel like idiots for wasting time and money on the class. If you run into a person like this, switch partners!

> **Me**: "I keep smelling roses and seeing a beautiful woman with long blonde hair. Do you have an Aunt name Rose on the other side?"
>
> **The Bad**: "What? Were you talking to me? Sorry I was checking Facebook."

The weekend came to an end, and that made me sad. It was a whirlwind of information and hands on experience that I am so grateful to have been a part of. And yes, I received my ATP certification!

What I Learned in Class

- Animal spirit guides are real, and they can appear in super-size!
- Etheric cords are real, and can be a little creepy.
- Oracle cards are a fun way to give readings when you combine them with your intuition. Always use your intuition.
- I love freebies!

Cards of Your Destiny
with William G. Bussey

After the ATP course, I took a five-month break. It wasn't intentional; there were just other things in my life taking priority. Travis started Little League, Sydney was busy in junior high, and I started belly dance lessons. I took a few in Arizona, but I was still a beginner. I looked forward to class each week for the music *and* the exercise. It felt magical dancing around the room to drum beats. My mind, body, and spirit were working together in harmony; it was a welcome change in my life.

I never spoke to anyone about my intuitive abilities except Kurt and the kids. I suppose it would have been great conversation if Peter was alive, but he wasn't. I didn't have a close relationship with my sister, so I couldn't share anything with her, and I already knew how the conversation with my mom would go:

> **Rena**: "Hey, Mom, how is it going?"
> **Mom**: "Hi, Rena. It's going. It has been really warm here—already in the 80s. What's new on your end?"
> **Rena**: "It has been really exciting! I attended a psychic development class last week where I levitated a man, moved objects with my mind, and grew a plant in my hand from a seed!"
> **Mom**: "That's nice. So how are the kids?"

By June of 2006, I was ready to hit some new classes. I found a one-day course at the Learning Light called Advanced Destiny with the 52-Card Playing Deck taught by William G. Bussey. It was held upstairs in one of the classrooms. I didn't attend the beginner class, but they let me in anyway.

It was really interesting. I still have the books and binder sitting on my bookshelf, and I don't plan on parting with them. As Bussey explained, you use a deck of playing cards found at any convenience store. The system employs similar concepts used in numerology, astrology, and the tarot to create a life path profile sheet, which contains your birth number card, planetary ruling card, and karma cards. This information is used to help you identify why you are here, why you have the life you have, challenges you may face, dynamics to relationships in your life, karma you brought with you, and many other things. If you enjoy working with numerology, astrology, and the tarot, I recommend this course.

In the class, I found out that my father and I were a lot more alike than I thought—ten of clubs, to be exact. I hate when that happens. I always thought that my dad gave really great advice, but he was tight with his money and believed that everything revolved around him. Maybe we were more alike than I wanted to admit—but definitely not the part about money.

> **Me**: "Hey, Dad, I need some money to buy new clothes. I'm down to one pair of pants, and they belong to Peter (I always wore his Levis)."
> **Dad**: "Do I look like I'm made of money? Do you know how much your clothes cost? Maybe if you had a job you could buy your own."
> **Me**: "Okay, just forget it."
> **Dad**: "Jeez, what is wrong with that kid? Man, I'm going to be late for my softball game, and it's my turn to buy pizza and beer afterward."

Maybe it was the 1970s mentality, because I heard similar stories from friends at school. Still, I don't remember them having to wear their brother's jeans.

The other thing that surprised me was that, according to the cards, Kurt was my destiny. This was according to his profile and mine. *I hate to throw a wrench in the cards of destiny, but we are divorced!*

I tried to explain to everyone that we were good friends, nothing else. But they didn't believe that mattered, because we had unfinished business, and he was my destiny in this lifetime. Eventually we would reconcile. My immediate thought was, *No! Been there, done that!* I took my notes on the subject and buried them. *What the hell do they know? It's just a stupid deck of playing cards!* Famous. Last. Words. Exactly one year later, Kurt and I moved in together.

What I Learned in Class

- A simple deck of playing cards can be a powerful oracle.
- Don't talk smack about the cards, especially when they can hear you.
- William G. Bussey is a genius. And so are his friends.

Touching Two Worlds
with Hollister Rand

After another long pause in my development, I took a one-day mediumship development class with Hollister Rand at the Awakenings Bookstore in Laguna Beach, California.

It was now February of 2007. I was still reading book after book in the evenings, but I hadn't had any hands-on training, and I was secretly worried that everything that I had learned would disappear. I was pretty excited to see her class listed on the bookstore's website.

Hollister was a small woman with a big personality. I could tell she had been doing her thing for a while and had answered every stupid question regarding mediumship ever asked. It was a small class, maybe twenty people. We worked through several exercises that day, primarily as a group, but there are two that stand out in my mind.

In one exercise, we worked with a pendulum. A pendulum is a weight on the end of a thin chain or string. The most common weights resemble the ones at the ends of arrows, and they are made from metal, gems, or crystal. The weights hang from a chain five to eight inches long. I once created one from a leather strap and a house key. It worked great—just ask Kurt about Stitch (our French bulldog). *Evil grin.*

Before you use it, you have to decide which way the pendulum should turn if the answer is *yes* or *no*. At times, it will turn in small circles, clockwise or counterclockwise. At other times, it will swing left to right or forward to backward. I like to keep things simple, up and down or clockwise for *yes,* left to right or counterclockwise for *no.* Once you set the intention with your pendulum, you are ready to get started.

To begin, you can hold the pendulum a couple of inches above a piece of paper, a desk, or a table. Clear your mind, ask your guides to assist if you want, take a deep breath, relax, and ask your question. As you wait, you may feel a slight increase in the weight of the pendulum as it begins to move. Remain steady; do not move your hands, wrists, arms, or any other parts of your body. Stay still and let the pendulum do the work. If it wobbles but stays pointing straight down, the answer may be unknown. It is best to keep your questions short and to the point.

Hollister gave a demonstration, and then the class worked individually with their pendulums to understand the process. After some practice, we came together as a group to watch each other ask questions and obtain results. I hate to say it, but it was painfully obvious that some of the other students were moving the pendulum themselves. *If I can see your arm and elbow moving, it's not the pendulum!* It was ridiculous. I think those people were working with their egos.

The second exercise took place after break. We were still sitting in a circle for group development work. Hollister led us through a meditation to relax our minds and get us ready to work with spirit. And then she shared a photo of a man with us. As we passed it around the room, she asked us to make note of any impressions or information we received from it.

When I held it, I saw big blocks of cheese, bottles and glasses of red wine, a long loaf of bread, and a stone balcony. I also felt a male presence. I wrote this all down and drew a picture of the balcony.

When everyone was ready, she went around the circle, one by one, asking us to share what we received. If you were right, she gave you a nod then moved on to the next person. If you were wrong, she told you.

When it was my turn, I shared the images with the group. "No, not what I'm looking for." She said. For a few moments, I sat there wondering what I was picking up if that wasn't it. As she moved around the circle, a student said, "Paris. I see Paris." She nodded, and then said, "Yes!"

It was a picture of someone she knew who passed away in Paris. Okay, I know I didn't say Paris specifically, but I got cheese, wine, bread, and a balcony. I think that's pretty close. I was pissed. I really don't remember anything else after that. From then on, I was riding the clock out until I could leave.

In truth, we all want validation, especially when we are still developing our skills. But we are not always going to get it while in class or while working professionally. We have to learn to trust what we get, no matter the outcome.

What I Learned in Class

- Trust what you get.
- People lie when using the pendulum.
- Sometimes I get moody in class.

Readers Studio with Terene

A few months after my last course, I found Readers Studio. It was a class held every Monday evening at the Learning Light Foundation. It was taught by Terene, one of the professionals that I had a reading with the week before. Terene's specialty was the tarot, and she wasn't really running a class—it was more like a weekly opportunity for us to give readings to the general public in a safe environment.

The Learning Light offered readings with advanced students for the affordable price of fifteen dollars for two fifteen-minute readings. It was a bargain, and the proceeds went to the Learning Light. There was a mix of experience levels in class: newcomers like me and students who had been giving readings for years. It was a two-hour class that began with a thirty-minute review of one of the tarot cards.

In the review, Terene shared various meanings that the card could have when it showed up in a spread, and we each shared our personal experience with it. And then Terene or one of the students would lead us through a short meditation to prepare us for the evening. After the meditation, we settled in at our individual tables while Terene unlocked the doors, reviewed the list of names on the sign-up sheet, and began ushering people in. If they didn't ask for a specific reader, she would select one of us for them.

Each reader selected specific divination tools for readings, such as oracle cards, tarot cards, or crystals. I used my favorite tarot deck, The Morgan Greer. I loved the bold pictures devoid of borders or words. I kept them wrapped in a white handkerchief with a small piece of amethyst and a clear quartz crystal to keep the energy clear. Later, I found a soft, black, cotton pouch with gold and red embroidery to carry everything in.

Some of the readers decorated their table with a tablecloth, unlit candles, crystals, bells, and small statues. I found some really cool material at the local fabric store and made a few tablecloths of my own. One was round and the other rectangular, so I had one for each type of table. This helped me set the stage and send a signal to my mind that it was time to give readings.

I was extremely nervous the first day. It was the first time that I gave a reading to someone for money. All the other readings were in class with other students. I definitely felt pressure—not so much to perform, but to help my client.

I said a silent prayer: *Dear guardian angels and spirit guides, please help me to hear the messages that I receive today for my readings. Please stay with me throughout the evening. Please keep all of us protected in white light and love. Thank you. I love and appreciate you so much, Amen.*

My first official reading was with a woman. She looked unkempt, like her hair hadn't been brushed for several days. She appeared to be clean but out of sorts as she sat down in the chair in front of me.

> **Me**: "Hi, I'm Rena. Can I have your first name?"
>
> **Client**: "Hi, I'm Kathy. I already know what I want to ask you about."
>
> **Me**: "Okay, I understand. If you don't mind, I would like to take a quick look at the cards. Sometimes, when we give an overall reading, the answer to the question is provided."
>
> **Kathy**: "Okay, sure."

She was a little off, that much I knew. I started feeling jumpy and dizzy. This was another side effect of becoming more intuitive: I was picking up feelings, emotions, and illnesses from people around me. And those sensations were magnified if I touched the person.

I have always been very empathic. It is something that I struggled with all my life. Walking into the mall or a grocery store was the equivalent of being beaten to death mentally. I felt light-headed, dizzy, and nauseous. Plus, I would get a pounding headache. It was terrible and drove my parents crazy. Luckily, using psychic protection consistently has completely changed that for me.

I shuffled the deck and spread the cards out in an arc face down on the table. "Kathy, please pick five cards and set them down in a face-down stack in front of you." As she did this, I stacked the remaining cards to my side with the crystal on top, and then I took the five cards she picked and laid them out face up.

When I looked at the spread, I kept seeing pictures of people— school pictures, snapshots, all sorts of images. I saw a medication bottle and a new home. This was not from the cards; rather, the information I received came from my *Clair Senses*.

Me: "Kathy, I'm going to begin sharing the information I am getting. Please give me a moment to get it all out before you ask questions. Sound good?"

Kathy: "Sure."

Me: "I see a new home, not new like it was just built, but new to you. Did you just move into a new home? Because if you did, it feels like a good fit for you. Maybe you were concerned. I also see medication and feel dizzy. Did you switch medications recently? Or did you discontinue a medication? I feel dizzy and a little light-headed." I paused a moment before I went on to discuss the pictures.

Kathy: "Yes, I did just move into a new home. I was really worried about the location, but so far it is working out really

well. I switched to new medication a week or so ago, but I stopped taking it because it was making me feel worse."
Me: *She said she stopped taking the medication, was this why I was feeling dizzy?* "I understand. I'm not a doctor, but maybe it would be a good idea to go back to the doctor and let them know. That way, they can help find the correct medication. It's up to you."

I was just about to tell her about the pictures I kept seeing when I heard Terene ring the bell. She did that to let everyone know that their fifteen minutes were up. As Kathy stood up, she showed me a ziplock bag she had in her purse. It contained dozens of pictures of family members, mostly her children at various ages. "I was really hoping to get a message about one of them today," she said. They were all still alive but not talking to each other. I felt horrible. I should have started the reading with the vision of the pictures instead of the house and medication. Maybe she would have received the message she was hoping for. We'll never know.

That was the hardest reading that I had given. It was even harder than standing up in front of a group of people, because someone was paying for it. I had a responsibility to them and myself.

After we finished for the evening, I sat with Terene to go over the evening's events. I was excited but drained. She assured me that what I was feeling was normal and would get better with time and practice. "Go home and get some rest, Rena," she said and smiled.

I packed up my things while I said a quick prayer to clear my energy field from any psychic debris. The last thing I wanted was for anyone or anything to follow me home. And then I said my good nights to everyone and went straight to the restroom to wash my hands, which I used as another way to disconnect from the energy of other people. I take psychic protection very seriously, and that includes cutting cords. So far, I haven't had any issues, and I really want to keep it that way!

After several months of giving readings consistently at the

Learning Light, my psychic abilities grew noticeably. It was awesome. I continued to ask for the clients' first names, but I no longer needed them to receive information. I really didn't need my tarot cards either; rather, I just had to look at the client and wait for the information to flow.

The first time this happened, I was sitting at my table waiting for my next client. I looked up to see a beautiful woman in her twenties walking toward me. As soon as our eyes met, images and words started flying around in my head: a cheerleader, football players, single, never married, no children, shy, and very quiet. When an average person looked at her, I don't think they would have those impressions.

She sat down and told me that she was deaf. That explained the feeling I received of her being very quiet. I smiled brightly at her, and then I grabbed the pad of paper to my left and acted like I was writing on it while looking at her. She nodded in affirmation—that would be our means of communication.

I began by writing, "What is your first name?" She wrote, "Cara. I have specific questions. Is that okay?" I replied, "Yes, of course. I already received some information about you, do you mind if I share it with you first?" She wrote, "No, please go ahead" and smiled.

> **Me**: Are you a cheerleader?
> **Cara**: Not anymore. When I was in high school.
> **Me**: Did you date a football player?
> **Cara** Yes!

At this point, I knew that he was part of one of her specific questions and that the information I received as she walked up was for her.

> **Me**: I feel that the relationship ended in high school, but
> he recently came back into your life.

Cara: Yes!

Me: I feel that he left abruptly, that you are worried that if you open yourself back up to him, he will let you down again.

Cara: Yes! What do you think? Should I trust him?

Me: I can't tell you *yes* or *no*. But I *feel* [here, I circled and underlined the word for emphasis] that he has changed, matured a lot, and thought of you often over the years. You will have to use your own intuition to determine whether you want to let him back into your life.

Ultimately, it is the client's decision. I can only tell them how *I feel*, the impressions that I receive. I can't make the decision for the client. Nor would I want to! Even if the guy felt like a mass murderer, she could still decide to date him for whatever reason. I share what I receive—that's all. It is up to the client to make the decisions that will impact his or her life. That is my philosophy, anyway. The last thing I need is some psychopath showing up at my door telling me that it is my fault that his or her girlfriend or boyfriend left.

My Monday night readings continued through the summer and into fall. By this time, Kurt and I had reconciled and were living together again as a happy family. I was feeling great about life, my family, and my intuitive skills.

One day, I was invited to give readings at the Learning Light annual Halloween bash. Initially, I was excited and felt honored to be a part of it. We were asked to dress up for the occasion, which was icing on the cake. Halloween was my favorite holiday. Don't get me wrong, Christmas is a close second—who doesn't like free gifts?—but nothing beats dressing up like someone or something for a whole evening. I had to come up with something good, something that spoke to me … and I knew exactly what it was. I dressed up as the Believe Faery, as created by Amy Brown. At that time, Amy was not only creating some of the most fascinating

Faery art, but she also had her own line of clothing called Faery Wear. I couldn't afford to by an outfit though, so I had to make my own. I found a pattern and some material at the local fabric store. After that, I found some fabulous wings at the Halloween shop. It turned out perfectly! I was a little overweight, but other than that, it looked good. As I was taking one last look in the mirror, Kurt stood next to me and said, "You look hot, babe." Kurt is always right!

The event was held in the main hall, on the first floor. There was a potluck in one of the classrooms for Learning Light members. The evening started off great. I gave several readings that went very well. Toward the end, I started feeling light-headed and dehydrated, so I took a break to grab a bite to eat and drink some water. While I was relaxing with some of the other members, I was told that Annette wanted to get a reading from me before I left. She was one of the professional readers I hadn't met. I had heard of her, but I had never seen her in person.

When my friend and mentor, Alex, told me this, my first thought was, *hell no!* One of the rumors I heard was that she changed her name to sound more authentic as a psychic (obviously not Annette). But since I was getting ready to leave anyway, I figured it would be ok. *What could go wrong?* Big mistake!

I finished my pizza, put on more lipstick, grabbed a piece of gum, and went back to my table. I was starting to feel better when she sat down in front of me—all five feet and eight inches of her jagged energy, which didn't include her hair. I wanted to run, but it was too late. "Hi, my name is Annette," she said as we shook hands. "I was hoping you could give me a reading before you left." I smiled and agreed, but I could tell that it was a bad idea. I began shuffling the cards as I said a quick prayer to myself, *Guardian angels and spirit guides, please help me get through this. Please don't leave my side. Thank you. Amen.* And then I laid the cards out in an arc.

> **Me:** "Please pick out five cards and stack them in front of you face down."

Annette: "You mean three cards, right? Five is too many
unless you are doing one of the larger spreads."
Me: "No, we need five cards for the spread that I use."
Annette: "Okay, but ...."

I used a tarot spread from the Llewellyn tarot called Lew's Spread.
It was one of two original spreads from the founder of Llewellyn
Publications, Llewellyn George. She was obviously not familiar with it.

I should have ended the reading there, but instead I took the
cards she pulled and laid them out into the spread. By the time I was
done, I had already received some images, thoughts, and feelings
about her. But as I listened more closely, I got nothing. Still, I didn't
panic, because I knew exactly what was happening.

Annette: "Maybe you need to go with a smaller spread,
maybe this one is too hard for you."
Me: "No, I use this spread all the time, it's not the cards,"
I said, looking straight at her.
Annette: "Obviously you are not getting anything. Too
bad. I heard you were really good. Maybe you are just off."
Me: *Did she really just say that?* "No, that's not it."
Annette: "I thought that you knew what you were doing.
We can just forget it."
Me: "No, I know what is happening."
Annette: "What?"
Me: "You are blocking me."

Judging from the look of complete disbelief on her face, I was
right. She was intentionally blocking me.

Annette: "What? No, I'm not."
Me: "Yes, you are. Every time you start talking, the
information starts flowing. Once you stop, it discontinues
and a wall goes up. You are testing me. Why?"

Annette: "No, you just aren't very good at getting information. That's not my fault."

Me: "I never said I was good to anyone. Why did you ask for a reading if you didn't want one? Who does that? This reading is over. I'm done."

I began putting my things away right in front of her. She just sat there staring at me. I was pissed off, it was late, and I wanted to go home and relax with my family. She realized I was serious, and then she flipped out again, demanding that I give her a reading. I kept my voice down while standing by my decision.

Me: "No, you need to ask someone else."

Annette: "But I wanted one from you." She said, trying to talk nicely.

Me: "Look, this isn't going to work. The energy between us is toxic."

Annette: "Can't you just try?"

Defeated, I sat back down while setting my bag in my lap and said, "No, but I will tell you what I have already received and you can figure out the rest. I got divorced, ex-husbands, sad, a boyfriend, and lonely." She stared at me in silence. Apparently, she was married and divorced several times, had a boyfriend, and was possibly sad and lonely. It may have been a good reading. Too bad for her.

To clarify, being blocked is not the same as getting nothing. There are times that, for whatever reason, we will not receive any information for a client. You will listen, but there will be nothing to pick up. When you are being blocked it *feels* different. It's like you can see the sun but you can't feel it, because it is blocked by the clouds. Getting nothing is as if the sun doesn't exist. Trust your instincts.

What I Learned in Class

- Consistent use of your abilities increases your psychic awareness and sensitivity.
- Always trust your instincts and intuition.
- Other readers can act jealous, even when you represent the same organization.
- There is more than enough to go around. Never be envious of another reader. Ever.

Soul Destinies Program with Robert Ohotto

After the Halloween incident of 2007, I took a long break unintentionally. The break lasted over a year. I say *unintentionally* because it wasn't planned; in fact, I planned to do the complete opposite. I wanted to stay involved with Readers Studio at the Learning Light for as long as I could. But something in me snapped after the reading with Annette; I felt burned out and frustrated with the process. It made no sense to expose myself to confrontation when all I wanted to do was be of service. I didn't want to see that person again or interact with her in any way. Because she was an icon there at that time, I decided to remove myself from the situation, which was really stupid in hindsight. Essentially, I was running away. While writing this book, that fact became obvious. And it was a pattern: whenever I faced adversity, I allowed it to become a personal roadblock that shut me down. My way of shutting down was to take myself out of the equation, but that meant I couldn't move forward with my intuitive development. I got really good at playing the victim during those episodes.

To stay tuned in, I continued reading about metaphysics, astrology, numerology, energy healing, runes, spells, and magic. I also meditated, kept up with my dream journal, and continued my automatic (unconscious) writing. I was hiding at home where I felt safe. And like always, the pang in my gut returned eventually.

When it did, I was reading a book called *Transforming Fate into Destiny: A New Dialogue with Your Soul* by Robert Ohotto. I loved the book, so I pulled up his website to check it out. Lo and behold, he had a class. And it wasn't just one class, it was a three-part program. They were all held at the Spearfish Canyon Resort in Lead, South Dakota. Each workshop was held on three days: Friday, Saturday, and Sunday. I signed up without hesitation.

Part one was originally scheduled in November of 2008, but there was a freak snow storm that hit the area really hard. Flights into South Dakota were canceled, and I was stuck in the Denver airport. The students who made it to the airport in South Dakota couldn't get a shuttle up the mountain to the resort, and the students who rented a car couldn't see three feet in front of them to drive. It was a nightmare. Thankfully, Robert and his team were able to reschedule the first class to a weekend in March of 2009. Part two took place in May, and part three occurred in October.

By the time part one came around in March, I was bouncing off the walls. Since I was working from home full-time, my interaction with people outside of my family was limited to the bartenders up the street at Red Robin. I also noticed that my sensitivity had increased. I think my ability to keep a barrier up had diminished substantially because I spent so much time alone. This wasn't limited to people; I was also sensitive to sights, sounds, and smells, which caused me to feel anxiety in restaurants, at the gym, in the mall, and at the grocery store. I felt nervous and self-conscious, and then the fight-or-flee syndrome kicked in, which was followed by hyperventilation and then fainting. It was terrible. Through trial and error, I found a secret weapon: a bottle of water. For some reason, holding and sipping a bottle of water grounded me. I learned to be prepared by carrying a bottle everywhere I went. There are about twenty half empty bottles rolling around in my car right now.

Robert's class was the first one that I attended after the anxiety began. I was worried, but I had faith that everything would work out. It had to.

Kurt dropped me off at the airport. He was visibly worried, but he gave me a ton of moral support and promised to keep the phone on him at all times. I made it through airport security without any problems, and then I went straight to McDonald's for a Diet Coke and a bottle of water. *So far so good,* I thought as I settled into an open seat at the gate and waited for my plane to come in. It was the first time I relaxed all morning. I was on my way to South Dakota!

The first half of the flight was right on schedule, and I spent my time reading. The second half of the flight was on a small plane that had two rows with two seats on each side. I sat next to a woman who looked about my age. We buckled in and prepared for takeoff.

As the plane started backing out of the gate, I looked down at her open tote bag by her feet and noticed Robert's book sitting toward the top. "Are you going to the class with Robert Ohotto?" I asked. "Yes. Are you?" She replied, with a cheesy smile that matched my own. "Yes!"

I introduced myself and found out her name was Mary. She seemed genuinely relieved to meet someone else on the same journey. I know I felt that way.

A few of the other passengers overheard us talking about Robert's book and joined the conversation. It turned out there were about seven of us on the same flight! Because we were scattered across the plane, though, I'm sure some of the other passengers were trying to figure out who the hell Robert Ohotto was!

My first impression of Mary was that she was an educated and well-spoken old soul. I felt lucky to be sitting by her because it relaxed me and gave me someone to talk to for the remainder of the trip. Oddly enough, I found out that she lived a few miles down the road from us and was on the flight with me from California. I made a mental note to pay more attention to my surroundings.

The flight went quickly. Those of us from class collected our luggage, and then we lined up for the shuttle van scheduled to take us to the resort. The ride took about an hour, including the winding two lane road up the mountain and through the forest. It was a beautiful drive, but I was slowly, steadily feeling weary. Between the airport, airplanes, and shuttle, I needed to disconnect, ground myself, and be alone for a while. I took out my bottle of water and drank, hoping that I wouldn't regret having a full bladder. I had no idea how much longer it would take, but I knew I could always ask the driver to pull over and go behind some bushes if I had to.

Eventually, we all started talking about movies. Something was said that reminded me of the movie *Hot Rod*. The main character is played by Andy Samberg. In the movie, he wanted to be a professional stuntman like Evil Knievel, but instead of a motorcycle, he rode a moped. Before his "big jumps," he called upon his animal spirit guides to assist him: the dolphin, the tiger, and the house cat. It's hilarious! As we talked about the movie, I began laughing so hard my eyes were watering. Mary had the same reaction. Between the water, the laughter, and a few partially opened van windows, I started feeling better.

We arrived at the resort in good spirits, but we were all hungry. We filed out of the van and into the lobby to get checked into our rooms. Several of the students were sharing a room, which was an option offered during registration. I reserved a room for myself, as did Mary. I felt uncomfortable sharing a room with a complete stranger. Also, I knew I needed a place to be alone. My room would become my sanctuary. It was a great decision.

After I checked into my room, I met up with Mary again for the meet and greet. The resort had a lodge look and feel that went perfectly with the forest surrounding it. There was a large sitting room for the guests to relax in that had a fireplace, various sofas, chairs, and pillows. It was a wonderful place to decompress with a drink after class.

Adjacent to the sitting room was a small conference room that had a table set up outside the door for class registration. We lined up to receive our name badges, custom three-ring binders filled with class materials, personalized natal charts based on our birth dates, and a box of oracle cards called Archetype Cards by Caroline Myss. We hit the freebie jackpot!

Mary and I sat down at one of the large, round tables in the room. They were serving light appetizers and nonalcoholic drinks. The bar area was just outside the door. We ate and introduced ourselves to the other students while waiting for Robert. Some of the students opened their boxes of oracle cards and began playing with them. It was a very large deck with vivid pictures that captured the essence of each archetype. Unfortunately, I had no idea what an archetype was. I could guess, but I was basically pretending I knew what everyone was talking about. They were also talking about Caroline Myss. Several of them had attended her courses. She sounded like a real hard-ass—a great instructor, but a real hard-ass. I was scared and made a mental note not to attend one of her classes for a while.

After a chunk of time passed, Robert came into the room. He was an attractive guy who looked like he had just stepped out of the hiking section of *Men's Health*. He was a well-spoken, quick-witted, dramatic man who displayed a hint of evil sarcasm. It was a good mix to keep my attention. *So far, so good.*

When the meet and greet ended, some of the students stayed at the bar to have a drink. I decided to stay sober and hit the sack. I had a lot of catching up to do with the whole Caroline Myss/ archetype thing.

We had breakfast in the restaurant located in a building across the lawn. It was also the building where our class was held. There was a large conference room attached to the dining room, which made it really convenient to grab a Diet Coke before, during, and after class.

As we gathered for the first time, I was surprised to see how many front-row seats were taken when we walked in. The tables were set up in long rows facing a small, raised stage in the front of the room. We had plenty of space to keep our binders open and cards out in front of us. There were large windows behind the stage with a view of the forest. There were also windows along the back where a table of refreshments and snacks was set up. Mary and I sat next to each other at a table about halfway back.

Class started with introductions by Robert and his wonderful staff. We got an overview of the schedule and a high-level review of the class materials that were entirely about astrology. *What? This class is about astrology? How did I miss that?* (For the record, that class remains the only class I registered for without knowing the subject matter.)

I looked around the room to see whether anyone else looked surprised. *Nope. No one. Just me … unless they have better poker faces.* By our first break, I knew that I was in over my head. They may as well have been speaking German, because I needed a dictionary to keep up. The level of astrology that I was familiar with was very basic, and this wasn't that.

"Mary, did you know that this class was going to be about astrology?" I asked reluctantly. She chuckled and replied, "Yes, didn't you?" My face said it all. Her smile was ear to ear, and I could tell she was trying to be supportive but really wanted to laugh.

Mary was an astrologer—not professionally, but she was extremely talented as I found out over the weekend. When I got lost or confused, I made a note and asked her about it at break or after class.

For those of you not familiar with astrology, it has a lot of moving parts and pieces such as houses, planets, signs, nodes, elements, and aspects. A natal (birth) chart is created using the date, time, and location that a person is born. Based on the planet, node, sun, and moon locations within the houses, interpretation of potentials and tendencies of people can be made based on those influences. It is not easy; it's complicated. Most people think astrology is only about the sun sign, but that isn't true.

There was a lot of information to learn at the foundational level. I wasn't disappointed, but I felt unprepared and a little blindsided. I thought I liked surprises, but I was wrong. I hate surprises.

In the first course (part one), we learned about the psyche, cosmic contracts, and the signs as archetypes, planetary archetypes, and astrological ages. According to the guidebook that comes with the archetype oracle cards deck, an archetype is a psychological pattern derived from a historical role in life such as mother, child, trickster, prostitute, or servant. With that being said, there was a lot of self-exploration that occurred over those three days. Yes, we were learning about astrology and how each planet, house, and sign worked in conjunction with the archetypes, but we were learning this by dissecting our own charts. This meant we were dissecting ourselves: our traits, habits, and issues. Were we victims? Were we prostitutes? Were we wounded children?

We were shining the light on all of those dark places within us that we didn't want to admit we had. And if by some chance we were aware of them, we sure as hell didn't want to go poking around in them. But we could no longer deny their existence. It was a frustrating, eye-opening, tiring experience. But to my surprise, it was also fun.

One evening during the weekend, we had a one-hour session that focused on a particular subject or archetype. Robert began with a discussion about the topic, followed by questions and answers and ending the evening with a guided meditation. After the meditation, we had an opportunity to journal the information we received. A lot of valuable insight came out of those mediations. Here are my notes after our mediation with the planet Saturn:

> Little boy, blond, wearing red suede shoes with white socks and shorts, named Troy. He took me to Notre Dame. We were sitting at the top of a large, stone building looking out over a marketplace. When I asked him about my path and direction, he motioned his arm and pointed out over the courtyard. Then Isis appeared. She was covered in gold with jewels on her wings. She lifted her wings, pointed, and said "Transformation it's time". But time for what?

I was going through a lot of personal transformation, still teetering on the fence about whether I should use my intuitive gifts professionally, overcome a host of self-esteem problems, and trying to bring forward and forgive all of my wounded child issues. There was a lot going on. And a lot more would surface before the end of the third workshop.

I also realized that I was a walking contradiction. Apparently, I looked like an extravert and spoke and acted with confidence. But I wasn't; I was shy and sensitive. Unlike my daughter, who was blessed with quick wit, a knack for evil sarcasm, and thick skin, I was the complete opposite. In fact, I'm still trying to find a comeback for something a woman said to me last week.

This could be confusing for people who didn't know me. It also made me a target. It's not that I'm a coward, but I don't have a good gray area. I'm either okay or ready to kick your ass. So if someone starts poking, I try to defuse the situation before stepping away to avoid confrontation. Some people view this as weakness, but in my view, I don't want to end up trying to explain to the police how my fork ended up in the side of someone's head. It's easier for me to play nice, even if what was said felt personal.

Over the year that I participated in the workshops, I only ran into two people who tested my nonexistent gray area. One of them was Rhonda.

During the second workshop, we worked in groups of two and three to read a natal chart that was being projected onto the screen in front of the class. Mary was on one side of me and Rhonda on the other.

Robert picked a group to share their reading with the class. In order for everyone to hear, one person in the group had to hold the wireless microphone as they spoke. Immediately, I tried to back out. "I would prefer not to do it. I hate the sound of my voice. I'm terrified of public speaking. Call me a chicken if you want," I confessed. They both laughed.

I got the impression that neither one of them was concerned, that either one of them would be fine speaking. So I relaxed. This was a bad idea because Robert picked us, and no one was up to the task.

Rhonda volunteered, but when she was given the mic, she kind of panicked and tried giving it to me. I shook my head, and then she switched personalities. In that nanosecond, her facial expression changed to a death stare, and her speech became direct and devoid of any emotion as she shoved the mic in my face.

I had a few choices: I could continue to say *no*, but this woman had crazy eyes. I'm not kidding: *crazy eyes*. They are not an urban legend. I knew I had to suck it up or stab her with my fork. And because there wasn't a fork nearby, I took the mic reluctantly and spoke. I sounded ridiculous. My voice was trembling as I read our notes and listened to the two of them remind me of all the details I forgot instantly when the mic touched my hand. But I did it. I faced my fear. Actually, I faced two fears: the mic and the crazy eyes.

After the exercise was over, I knew I needed to distance myself from Rhonda to avoid any future confrontation. If I moved seats, she would want to know why and an argument would follow, so I acted like nothing happed. It felt like crap.

I spoke to Mary about it when we had a few minutes alone. She didn't hear what was said, so she couldn't really comment. But it sparked a great conversation about personal boundaries.

"Rena, you really need to create some boundaries for yourself. If you don't, you will continue to get bounced around like that," she said.

"What do you mean?" I asked.

Mary explained that, by establishing personal boundaries between me and other people, it sets the expectation of what is and is not acceptable. That way, I'm not just taking it all in and feeling horrible about myself for weeks to come. The advice aligned with everything I was learning that year. I played the victim a lot, much more then I wanted to admit. In short, I needed to find that middle ground.

From that day on, finding the middle ground has been a work in progress. I can stand my ground without being rude or mean, and I can keep the peace without selling myself out.

By the end of the third workshop, I was using what I learned about mediumship and the *Clair Senses* and applying them to the astrological chart interpretation exercises.

Robert shared a chart on the screen that we were instructed to read. And then he would open the floor for us to raise our hands and share our readings of it. It was fun.

As I did this in my head, I noticed that I began to receive information about the individual not contained in the chart. I was using my *Clair Senses*. As people began to read the charts out loud, I found that I was correct a large portion of the time. It felt like I was back in Readers Studio.

I was hesitant to share my readings with the class because I didn't know how to link the information I received back to the chart. Plus, I didn't want to be wrong in front of all the budding astrologers. But then I changed my mind—what a mistake. I said something like, "Based on the planet alignments within the houses, I feel like this person is lonely but has family. Like there is a mother figure that is missing. She is independent but needs nurturing."

I wanted to say more, but I couldn't get it out fast enough before Robert asked what everyone else thought. This is when Mary explained to me what was really going on in the chart. After that, several other students restated what I had already said. I hate when that happens. I just sat there with a fake smile.

Robert asked the young woman who the chart belonged to for validation of the information. She said she was independent and had been on her own from a young age. Her mother passed away, but she was adopted by her aunt who was nice but not her mother. Lately, she needed to hear her mother's voice and to feel her love and support in her life.

I was on the right path, but I didn't get it from the data in the chart. This is when I acknowledged that, regardless of the tool I used, the main way I received information was through my *Clair Senses*, the chakras, the auras, and from spirit. The tool was just a starting point to get the information flowing.

2009 was a year of self-discovery. I met wonderful people that I still stay connected to via Facebook. And that includes Robert, who was one of the funniest instructors I have had so far, a man who spent time talking to us individually.

I didn't expect to learn astrology that year, but I did. I didn't expect to learn about the archetypes, but I did. There is no doubt that it was no accident; I was meant to be there, meant to learn about my psyche, meant to learn about myself.

What I Learned in Class

- Take a chance by learning something new.
- Trust what you get. Never let anyone but the receiver tell you that you are wrong—and even they have brain freeze sometimes.
- Remember to set your boundaries. Love yourself enough to put yourself first.
- Finish what you start. I understand that life can get in the way, but the payoff is worth it.
- Remember to stay away from people with crazy eyes!

Mastering Mediumship
with James Van Praagh

I continued to study astrology on my own, adding a plethora of new books to my shelves. But it was time to get out again, so I started surfing the Internet in search of something local. *Ask and you shall receive,* I thought when I found a three-day workshop a few freeways away. It was the advanced mediumship Course with James Van Praagh, held at the Aliso Creek Inn in Laguna Beach, California. It was scheduled for August of 2010, almost a year after my last workshop with Robert Ohotto.

When the weekend came, I couldn't wait to get going. Because it was an advanced mediumship class, I was even more excited. Plus, it was the first time I was going to see James in person. The class being so close to home and right across from the Pacific Ocean was an added bonus. There was no travel stress; I could just enjoy class and sleep in my own bed at night.

The class was held in a large conference room in the main building of the resort. Tables were set up outside the double doors for registration. I received my name badge, a medium-sized spiral notebook, a pen, and a cloth bag to hold everything. I think I also received a water bottle to stay hydrated.

As I walked into the room, I heard pop music playing. The chairs were set up in big circles, all facing each other. It was a large class of about seventy-five students. There was a small stage in the front and windows along one side with a view of the golf course.

I immediately recognized a younger guy who was in Robert's class the year before. I think he worked as the sound and equipment technician for the event. His name was Max. I went over, gave him a hug, and asked, "Are you working?" He wasn't; he was there as a student this time. Robert's class must have sparked his curiosity. It was a quick conversation because I wanted to get situated within the circle across the room.

James stepped into the room from a set of doors by the stage. Everyone began applauding as he grabbed the mic and began his introductions. They were followed by a brief overview of the class schedule and hotel layout.

We must have looked a little too serious or nervous when that was done, because he said, "Everyone on your feet! Come on, on your feet!" We all stood up as music started jamming out of the speakers. James was bouncing up and down to the beat. "Let's go! Time to loosen up!" We danced around, trying not to look at each other for fear of laughing to death. I was more than a little self-conscious. I'm sure if Sonia was there she would have been proud to see me get out of my ego.

There was a noticeable difference in the room when the music stopped: it was much lighter. It's funny that I didn't notice it was heavy before. I guess the dancing worked. And I'm sure the laughing didn't hurt either.

We settled back into our seats as James went through a review of the *Clair Senses,* chakras, and auras, followed by our first break. When we came back, James explained our first exercise. By this time, I had met a like-minded woman from out of town named Debbie. She was one of those people that you feel like you have known your whole life. There was no effort required to befriend her, and conversation came so easily that I forgot we just met. She was recently separated, and like me, she had been on the workshop circuit for the last five years.

For the first exercise, we were asked to pair up with someone in our circle. Debbie and I chose each other and moved our chairs to the side of the room for privacy. Our readings went well. There was nothing astounding, but we both received information for each other that we had not shared yet. It helped boost our self-confidence for the readings to come.

There was a good mix of professional and aspiring mediums like myself. It was a nicely balanced class where everyone was wholeheartedly participating.

During one exercise, James had us stand up and create two rows of two chairs facing each other. "Everyone pick a seat," James instructed. "We are going to do speed readings on each other," he explained, causing us all to chuckle. "Everyone in the rows facing the window, when I say *start*, you are going to read the person in front of you. Then, when I say *switch*, you are going to stand up and move to the chair to your right. The people in the rows facing the wall will stay put. Got it?" We all nodded and prepared ourselves. I was just a bit giddy because I was the reader. "We will continue to do this until I say *stop*. Then we will take a few minutes to reset and switch roles. Ready?" James asked.

Because these were speed readings, we were encouraged to share everything we received as fast as we could. This meant there was no time to filter or question things prior to sharing them. We just got everything out as fast as we could, only pausing long enough for a yes or no from the receiver.

I was trying not to freak out as I waited for James to tell us to start. I said a quick prayer: *Dear guardian angels and spirit guides, please be with me and whomever I am reading. Please help me to be a clear channel for the information that I receive. Please give me the strength to communicate the information clearly to the receiver. Please let the messages that I receive only be for the highest good for everyone involved. I love and appreciate you all. Amen.*

The next thing I knew, James said, "Start!" My heart was racing as I tried to establish a connection with the woman sitting across from me.

Me: "Hi, I'm Rena, what is your first name?"

Woman: "Hi, I'm Katie."

Me: "Hi, Katie. As soon as you said your name, I felt a grandmother presence. Do you have a grandmother on the other side?"

Katie: "Yes."

Me: "Great. I can see a white house, wooden, with a front porch. It reminds me of my husbands' grandparents' home in Iowa on the farm. Did she live on a farm?"

Katie: "Yes."

Me: "Did her house look like that?"

Katie: "Yes."

Me: "I see her in an apron, full length. Was she known for her baking?"

Katie: "Yes."

Me: "I can see a pie sitting in an open window to cool off."

Katie: "Yes, she loved to bake pies!"

By this time, I could see her grandmother clearly. She was sitting down in a chair and holding a muffin, but the muffin was about the size of a large football. I wasn't sure what it meant, but I had to share it with Katie: "I see your grandmother sitting in a large chair. She is holding a muffin, but the muffin is really big." I held my hands out in front of me about twelve inches apart. "Do you know what this means?" Katie started laughing and nodding her head up and down. "Yes, my grandma had a dog she absolutely loved about that big, and she always sat on my grandma's lap. Her name was Muffin." We both started laughing. I went on to relay the love, support, and advice that her grandma shared with me in that very short period of time.

This is one of my all-time favorite readings. I've shared it with dozens of people when they ask me how mediumship works. It breaks the ice and lets a little humor into the discussion, especially for the skeptics. Plus, it always reminds me to share what I get no matter how ridiculous it seems. Our job is to be the channel for the information to flow through, like a telephone. If we filter something out, we may be removing a large piece of the evidential information critical to the receiver. It could be that one piece that they needed to hear in order to move on and heal.

When we came in the next morning, the chairs were set up in rows facing the stage with one main aisle down the middle. "I wonder if we are going to have to stand on stage and give a reading," I said to Debbie, who had just come in with a fresh cup of coffee. "Wow, already? It seems really quick, right?" she replied. I nodded while taking another long swig of my Big Gulp. *It isn't going to be me.* My armpits started sweating just thinking about it.

Saturday was the full day, and it was packed with exercises from beginning to end. Early on, James asked us to provide him with pictures of loved ones that had passed away. If we didn't have a picture, we could provide him with a piece of our jewelry. The objects would be used for readings over the next two days. I didn't have a picture, so I gave him a bracelet that I wore all the time.

In one exercise, James walked us through a meditation to open our chakras and journey back to before we were born, back to when we were still in our mother's womb. There was soft music playing in the background as we relaxed. And then James instructed us to tune into what we were experiencing. "Can you hear your mother's voice? Can you taste anything? How do you feel? Sick? Happy? Sad? Are you feeling your emotions or your mother's?" he asked.

As I listened to him, I could feel my mother's anxiety and sadness. She wasn't ready for a second child. She felt trapped, helpless, and hopeless. It broke my heart. I could also taste cigarette smoke. It was as if I were the one holding the cigarette and taking a drag.

James then began bringing us back to the present, slowly guiding us awake. When I opened my eyes, I started to cry. I already knew I was an accident.

Years earlier, I asked my mom whether my little sister (who

is seven years younger) was an accident. She said, "No, *you* were the accident. I was on the pill when I got pregnant with you." It all made sense, but that didn't make it any easier. We always had a distant relationship. We were never close when I was growing up, and we never hung out together when I got older like she did with my little sister. I guess it all started the day she found out she was pregnant with me.

Thirty minutes ago I was happy, now I really need a drink.

James walked up and down the aisle asking questions about our experiences while giving the wireless mic to the person speaking so we could all hear. "So did anyone taste anything?" he asked. I was sitting in an aisle seat, so I was easy to see. Without thinking, I said, "Yes." He came right up to me and put the mic in front of my mouth.

If you are like me, you don't like the sound of your own voice, especially when it is being broadcast across the room on a loud speaker. I immediately pulled my head back a little bit, but it didn't help, because he just stepped forward to push it closer so everyone could hear me. It was an awkward struggle. "Cigarettes. I tasted cigarettes," I said, trying not to hear my own voice. "Yes," James said as he looked around the room. "This is common." And then he moved on to the next person.

He was three questions on before my heart finally came down from my throat and back into my chest. It was another few questions before my heart stopped beating so quickly. It was ridiculous. *How can I become a successful medium if I don't like the sound of my own voice?* I was sure that there were CDs I could listen to or a class I could take to help me with it, and I knew that, if all else failed, therapy was always a good option. For the moment, I just had to avoid being called up on stage.

Later in the day, we began working with the photos that James collected from the class. There were many working mediums in the class who made a point to let James know who they were. Unlike wusses like me who would have kept it to myself unless directly asked, they put it out there for everyone to scrutinize over the next day and a half. My guess is they thought that, once they proved to James how amazing they were, he would help propel them into superstardom.

Unfortunately for one of them, the opposite occurred. She was a young woman dressed in black with hair that matched. I never had a chance to speak to her, but she appeared to have a good, upbeat personality. The bad news is that she wasn't a good medium.

James gave her several opportunities, but she continued to be wrong. I don't remember her getting one validated message the whole time she was on the stage. To add a bit more drama, she argued with him, which only made things worse and harder for us to watch. They were both becoming visibly frustrated when the conversation got real.

> **James**: "Did you say you did this professionally?" he asked, staring right at her with an astonished look on his face.
> **Woman**: "Yes," she said, staring back at him.
> **James**: "So you charge people for your readings?" he asked.
> **Woman**: "Yes," she answered defensively.
> **James**: "I can't believe that they are satisfied based on what we have seen here today," he said with his hands on his hips.
> **Woman**: "But I'm usually really good," she said, looking around the room.
> **James**: "You may want to consider pulling back for a while. Maybe take a break from giving readings professionally until you have more experience," he said with equal parts compassion and concern.

By this time, the room was humming with side conversations. But my eyes were fixed on the conversation taking place on stage. I felt genuinely bad for her, but he was right: she appeared inexperienced, and an inexperienced medium running around could be bad for everyone's private practice, not just hers.

After he asked her to sit back down, he took the opportunity to talk to the class about ethics, standards, and the importance of qualification before starting a business. I'm sure it was a hard lesson for that gal to learn publicly, but at least it was in a class and not a bad review on social media.

As we moved on, James took out a picture from the ones he collected from the class. It was of a young boy, maybe fourteen years old. He was a good-looking kid who reminded me of my son. James picked one of the students who volunteered to come up and give a reading for it on stage.

As the woman held the photo, she began to receive the boy's name, the first letter, the sound. It was confirmed by the mother in the class. As the woman continued, I started getting impressions of my own: a BMX bike, skateboards, wooden ramps. I also saw a group of young boys getting high on marijuana using an empty soda can as a pipe. I sat there taking it all in, wondering if it was really him. And then I could *feel* him. He was very close to his mom; he loved her very much and was worried about her. He was a wonderful son, a great kid, a companionate kid who was good to others. He played sports like baseball and football. He was also the kind of kid that would stop a bully—just an all-around good kid.

After this download, I started to tune into the woman on stage giving the reading. She began painting a picture, touching on a few of the things that I had already picked up. When she was done, James asked the boy's mother to validate the information for the class. But before she even spoke, I could hear a loud, annoying noise. It was crazy. I looked around, but no one else appeared to be distracted by it. It continued to get louder and louder until I finally figured out what it was. It was the sound of a skateboard rolling across wood, the sound of wheels rolling across wooden ramps lifted off the ground! The wheels created a hollow, grinding sound, followed by a loud bang from the skateboard crashing down.

The boy's mother explained that her son was very athletic, but he had passed away under the influence of drugs while skateboarding with friends. She also said that he had a wonderful personality, that he was a great son, a giving kid, never selfish. She was struggling with overwhelming sadness since his death. I wanted to tell her he was there, right next to her, but I didn't have to. James was already on top of it. He let her know that her son was doing very well on the other side, helping other kids his age that recently crossed over to adjust to their new environment. He missed her dearly, but he needed her to move on and heal. He was worried about her overall health and well-being. It was a beautiful reading.

Our last day of class ended at noon. We spent the morning pairing up for readings and continuing with the platform mediumship practice. (And yes, I successfully dodged that bullet.) By the last hour, a group of us had gathered toward the back of the room, relaxing, joking, having a good time, and listening to the other readers on stage. When it was over, the bag of pictures and jewelry collected the day before was circulated around the room for everyone to reclaim their belongings. One of the women in class took the time to pull things out and hold them up for easy identification.

A picture of a gentleman in his sixties was passed to me to pass to a woman in back of me. I opened my hand for the woman to place it on my palm as I pivoted around in my seat to face the lady behind me. During those few seconds, I received a stream of images and feelings. I saw antique cars, a crystal ashtray, and a funny man, and I heard the word *daughter. Was she his daughter and took after him?*

When she picked the photo up from my hand, I asked her if the picture was of her dad. "Yes," she answered, looking surprised.

"Did he work for a car dealership?" I asked. And then she started smiling.

"Yes, he did."

"Did he work in the corporate offices? Was he a smoker?" I asked the questions as I stared at her intently.

"Yes, he was a very heavy smoker back in those days."

"Did he collect antique cars or want to?"

"Yes, he loved them. He couldn't afford them, but he knew all about them. Is he here? Are you connecting with him?"

Unfortunately, I wasn't. Still, I had the strong sense that he missed her and their long conversations, so I shared what I had. It felt more psychic than mediumship, but she seemed happy. Sometimes, a little bit of something is better than nothing.

The class came to a close on time. There was book signing and pictures with James, but I didn't participate in either activity.

One thing I haven't mentioned is something I saw on the second day of class, while James was up on stage talking. I kept seeing a man dressed up in a pink tutu with black Converse high-tops, a crown, and a magic wand. At first, I thought he was supposed to be a prom queen of some sort. But then I realized that he was actually playing Glinda the Good Witch from the Wizard of Oz. He was jumping up and down behind James, having a great time mimicking him. If I had to guess, I would say that it was a friend of his, and that a group of them dressed up as the characters from the Wizard of Oz one Halloween. I thought about sharing what I saw with James, but it didn't seem like a good idea. I'm sure he has his share of students trying to prove themselves to him over the years, and I didn't want to annoy him. Was it real? Was I making it up? I guess we will never know.

What I Learned in Class

- Don't open a private practice until you have sufficient training and experience.
- Money should not drive your ambition to become a professional medium—being of service should. If you make a ton of money at it, consider it a bonus.
- Don't brag about your abilities to your instructor.

Deepen Your Connection with Spirit with Lisa Williams

Three months after my weekend workshop with James, I attended a two-day intensive mediumship workshop with Lisa Williams at the Embassy Suites in Dallas, Texas. I had seen Lisa on TV and read her book, *Life Among the Dead*. So, when I found out that she was teaching a workshop, I wanted to go. But not long after I registered for the class, the feeling started to wear off.

As the day came closer, the feeling became stronger, but I didn't know why. Still, there was no way I was going to waste the money I spent on tuition and flights. *It's only two days; I can handle it,* I thought. From what I had seen and read, Lisa was a quirky, funny chick from the United Kingdom. How could it not be fun?

As I walked up to the front desk of the hotel to check in, I could smell cigarette smoke. "Is this a nonsmoking hotel?" I asked the women processing my paperwork. "No, we have rooms that are available for smokers. You can also smoke in the bar." *Oh no ...*

I apologize to any smokers reading this, but when you are a nonsmoker, the smell of cigarettes is really foul. It sticks to your hair and clothing and gets into your system, which forces you to taste it. This wasn't a complete deal breaker, but it wasn't a good sign either.

The first day of class started off pretty well. At registration, outside the conference room, we received a small writing journal, a pen, and a cute travel candle that I still have today.

When I walked into the room, I saw that there were several round tables set up in the back and two main rows of chairs set up facing the stage with an aisle running down the middle. I took a seat in the back row.

Lisa began with introductions followed by a brief overview of what to expect in the class. After that, we began our first exercise: the memory game.

"Please have a seat at one of the tables in the back, pick a partner sitting next to you, and then open the box and begin setting up the pieces," Lisa instructed. We followed her directions as I prayed that we weren't going to play the *actual* memory game created for small children that could be purchased at any local toy store. But I was wrong.

For those of you unfamiliar with it, the memory game consists of a deck of cards that has pictures on one side. To begin, you lay all of them out face down on the table. The first player will select two cards. If the pictures match, he or she continues to select two cards at a time until an unmatching pair is selected. If the cards don't match, they're turned face down. After that, the second player takes his or her turn. The player with the most pairs wins. This wasn't exactly what I thought I was spending my hard-earned money on, but I didn't have much choice.

My partner was a heavy-set, middle-aged woman who wouldn't stop talking. She claimed that she had surgery recently that hindered her ability to remember things, but nobody at the table believed her.

Everyone looked really disappointed during this exercise, except for the woman sitting next to me. She had turned the ridiculous exercise into an all-out competition. I wanted to remind her that we weren't participating in a game show, but it wouldn't have done any good. She was on a roll that was making me and the other six students at the table uncomfortable. She even critiqued the way

I turned the cards over. I kept my boundaries, but I also tried to keep things light-hearted for the sake of everyone at the table. Each time I looked up, I got the we-are-so-sorry-you-are-stuck-with-her look from the other students. It was painful. She was almost out of breath at one point due to her excitement. *I'm so done,* I thought. It was obviously a beginner-level class, but it had just started, and my patience was already at zero.

When we returned to our seats, I made sure I sat as far away from that woman as possible. I cleared my energy, silently recited a prayer of protection, and cleared my thoughts for the next exercise. As the class went on that day, so did the repetition of all the things I had learned over the last six years. It was all review, nothing new. My boredom and disappointment were epic. I was going to leave after the first day, but Kurt talked me into staying.

"Babe, I'm coming home. This sucks," I mumbled.

"Rena, it's just one more day. You said it yourself: you always learn something new or have a breakthrough in each class," he said.

"But this is a beginner class, and I can't stand it. I should have paid more attention to the class description. From now on, I need to stick with advanced-level courses," I replied, completely defeated.

"Just one more day, Reen, then you don't have to pay for a flight change." He was right. The last thing I wanted to do was waste more money on this trip, so I hung up and went to bed.

The next day went just like the first. I was having a really hard time changing my attitude until Lisa did something really cool that made it all worth it.

The topic was auras, and the exercise was how to see them around people and things. This included spirit energy. Lisa used herself as an example and stood in front of the class.

Per Lisa's instruction, a student turned off the lights in the back of the classroom. Lisa was standing directly in front of a white wall with her arms out to her sides, palms facing forward and feet shoulder-width apart. She closed her eyes, took a few deep breaths, and called in her spirit guides and loved ones on the other side.

Suddenly, we could see several shadows of people all around her on the wall! As we continued to watch, more of them appeared.

At first, I assumed what I was seeing was *our* shadows on the wall, but it couldn't be us based on the lighting. Plus, they were moving independently of us!

Lisa began to close down by thanking her guides and loved ones for coming. While she was speaking, the shadows began to disappear one by one, leaving just her shadow behind. ***Wow!*** It was the coolest thing ever!

When we came back from our afternoon break, I sat next to a guy in one of the back rows who had the same look on his face that I felt inside. His name was Tony. I found out that he was basically in the same situation as I was. He was fried from all the workshops, wondering what to do with all the knowledge and experience that he had gained over the years. "Should we become professionals? Why do we keep coming back for more when we could spend all of this money on an actual vacation?" He asked. I didn't have the answer.

As we sat there commiserating, it became clear that I wasn't alone. There were many of us on this journey trying to figure out where we fit in and how.

I stayed in class until it was time to head to the airport. I had my bag with me, so when the time came, I stood up quietly, gave Lisa a big smile, and mouthed *thank you* before leaving.

Lisa was every bit as awesome as I expected her to be. If I were a beginner, it would have been a great experience.

What I Learned in Class

- It was time to take a break.
- I needed to stick with advanced courses.
- Kurt was right: I always learned something new in class.

Psychic Forensics with Nick Sutcliffe

Six months later, I began attending a weekly psychic forensics class at the Learning Light Foundation with Nick Sutcliffe. It was April of 2011, and they had new classes and new instructors. Fortunately, Annette was no longer one of them. The energy in the place felt completely different; it felt much lighter than before. I breathed a sigh of relief that my nemesis was gone.

This was the first time that I met Nick. He was a professional healer at the Learning Light who had been using his intuitive gifts for over thirty years. He was a big guy who reminded me of Russell Crowe.

I didn't know what to expect in class, but the description sounded awesome. Secretly, I was hoping to assist in a missing person's case. As it turned out, one of the first exercises we did entailed locating a woman's stolen cell phone. It wasn't exactly a *person*, but it was still really cool. She was a friend of Nick's who had asked him for our assistance.

We started off using a series of techniques to identify the person who took the phone and find out where it was currently located. First, Nick walked us through the scenario of where the phone was last seen: a grocery store in New Mexico. Next, he asked us to open ourselves up to that location and make note of any impressions we received.

There were no prior meditations or prayers of protection. That was something we did on our own, not something we did as a class. That method worked well, though, because we all had our own beliefs. Consequently, I said my usual prayer of protection, begging my guides to stay close and asking them to help me to stay open to the information that I received. I also asked Archangel Michael to protect us all from anything negative. When I was done, I took a few deep breaths and relaxed my mind.

Slowly, I started seeing a young man, a teenager—maybe seventeen or eighteen years old. He looked Hispanic, tall, and thin. He had short hair and was wearing a pair of Converse high-tops. As I made note of the details of his appearance, I began to *feel out* the situation. It felt like the phone wasn't stolen; rather, it was *found* in the produce section of the grocery store. The person who found it never turned it in. I finished my notes before we moved on.

Our next exercise entailed identifying the current location of the phone. Nick gave us each a printout of a map of the area and a pendulum. "To begin," he said, "I want you to take your dominant hand and hover it above the map, palm down. After that, slowly glide it across. If you feel a warm spot or a shift in energy, circle it on the map." We nodded in agreement and began following his instructions.

Interestingly, I could feel the heat over one specific area in the upper right corner, so I took my pencil and circled that area. To make sure I didn't miss anything, I did it again. I held my right hand over the map—back and forth, up and down—but the warm spot remained the same.

When the class was done identifying the location, Nick said, "We are going to do the same thing, but this time we are going to use the pendulum." Once again, we all nodded in agreement and picked up our pendulums.

"To begin, hold it over the middle of the map and ask it to point to the current location of the cell phone. Give it a few moments to respond. If nothing happens, begin moving it to different locations on the map and ask it whether that is the current location. Ask it to respond either by turning in a circle clockwise for *yes* or counterclockwise for *no*." After Nick answered a few questions, we began working individually with our pendulums.

I held my pendulum right above the middle of the map. In my head I asked, *Please point to where the cell phone is.* I could feel my hand starting to get warm, and then I felt a slight tug on the end of the pendulum as it stiffened. Slowly, the point began to move to one side about a half an inch, and it pointed toward a city on the map. It was the same area that I had already circled! I whispered a thank you to my pendulum as I moved it directly above one of the cities that I circled.

"Is this where the cell phone is?" I asked. It responded immediately by turning in a counterclockwise circle, meaning *no.* So I moved it a bit to the right until it hovered atop the next city. I then asked the question again. This time, it responded by turning in a clockwise circle, meaning *yes.* I whispered, "Thank you." I then circled the city name on the map. When the class completed the exercise, we compared the locations that we identified. Almost all of us circled the same area.

Many months went by before the authorities were able to track down the cell phone, but our information turned out to be correct. They verified that the phone was found (not stolen) in the produce area of the grocery store. In fact, an employee found it. He also fit the description we provided. He sold the phone to another person, and the police tracked him down. Because the phone was reported stolen, the police forced the man to return it to the owner. I guess that's the downside to buying stolen property.

One day, we entered the classroom and found a stack of dowsing rods sitting in the middle of the table. I bought a pair years ago but never took them out of the packaging. I was pretty excited to see them. I wondered what we were going to be searching for. Nick asked us to pick out two rods and set them down beside us. It was hard to avoid playing with them.

He began class by explaining that we were going to be looking for a couple (a man and a woman) who were lost in the garden. That didn't make any sense to me, because the garden wasn't very big.

He handed us each a sealed envelope. "Don't open it," he said. "To begin, I want you to hold it in your hands and write down any impressions you receive from it. What does the couple look like? What color is their skin? Are they tall or short? Are they young or old? Do they wear glasses? Write it all down."

I held the envelope between the palms of my hands and took a few deep breaths to clear my mind. "Who are you?" I asked to myself. I started getting small impressions of the woman first. She was short with dark hair. I thought she might be Asian. Next, I saw the man, but he kept turning into Nick. No matter how many times I cleared the impression out, it just kept coming back. I could also taste cigarette smoke. I started to write the description, but I felt awkward doing it because I was basically describing Nick.

Next, Nick handed us each a map of the garden outside. It was a fenced in area that was part of the Learning Light. It had several sitting areas, flowers, trees, and shrubs.

"Slowly hover your dominant hand, palm down, across the map. If you feel warmth or a shift in energy, place a big *X* on that area on the map. There are five hidden pictures of the couple in the garden, so try to identify five areas on your map."

Eagerly, we began hovering our hands over our maps. We knew we were getting one step closer to playing with the dowsing rods. "Please show me the location of each of the pictures that are hidden in the garden," I asked the map. I took a few deep breaths to clear my head and extended my hand over the map, slowly moving it in a large circle. I began to feel warm spots. They stuck out like invisible bumps and were sprinkled across the garden. I isolated them one by one, placing a big *X* on each location. I was feeling pretty good about the energy moving through me, and I wanted to get out there as soon as possible.

"Okay, let's begin with the photo of the missing couple," Nick said. "Who wants to go first?" Not me. I waited until a few of the other students raised their hands. One by one, we went around the table. While they were talking, I was making a mental note of all the attributes they shared that were the same as mine (along with the ones that were different). Things came out about even. The ones that were different centered on the woman in the photo. She seemed to be giving everyone a problem.

When it was my turn to share, I started with the woman: "I can't get a clear read on her age, but she feels like late thirties, dark hair, light skin, brown eyes, petite, not tall or heavy." I looked over at Nick but got nothing. He is a master of the poker face, a cool character who never gives anything away, which makes him a perfect instructor. I smiled and went on.

"The male was even more challenging because I kept seeing a man who looked just like Nick," I said. Again, he had no change in expression. "He wore gold rimmed glasses and smoked. I could taste it."

The last student had the same impressions that I did: he kept seeing a picture of Nick. One of the other students said that the woman resembled Nick's girlfriend, who was also an instructor at the Learning Light.

"Open your envelopes," Nick said. We all ripped into them like it was Christmas morning. Immediately, we all began laughing as we pulled out a picture of Nick and his girlfriend. It was such a relief because it was driving a few of us crazy.

I had identified the high-level description of his girlfriend, but nothing else. Some of the other students didn't get her description, but they wrote down that she was an unmarried teacher and psychic. I was a bit disappointed, but I was happy that I identified the man as Nick.

After we took a short break, it was time to play with the dowsing rods. "If you haven't already picked out a pair of dowsing rods, please do so now," Nick instructed. As a few of the students did that, the rest of us played with ours.

The dowsing rods were just like the ones I had at home: they were made of thin metal in the shape of an L. We were instructed to hold them as if they were guns. The handle is about five inches long, and the long part that points forward is about ten inches long. There is a thin, clear plastic guard on the handle that allows the dowsing rod to swivel left and right while you hold it. This can be tricky when you are using them outside if there is a slight breeze.

"Is everyone familiar with how to use the rods?" Nick asked. We all nodded. "Okay, then let's get started," he said and smiled. As he got up from his chair, he said, "Everyone, grab your dowsing rods."

Nick provided a demonstration before we went outside. He held a rod in each hand, about ten inches apart, and made them align in a parallel position. "Make sure you hold the rods parallel to the ground as you ask them to show you where the photos are, and then wait for their response," he said as he looked up to make sure we were paying attention. We were. "You might feel a slight shift in energy as the rods turn left or right."

"What if they stay straight ahead, pointing forward?" one of the students asked. "Then you can move forward until they cross like this," Nick replied as he caused the rods to cross in front of him intentionally. "Once they cross, look around that immediate area for the envelope. Are there any questions?" We had some, but we decided to work them out while we were playing in the garden. "Okay, remember to keep them parallel to the ground. Don't let them point up or down, and keep them eight to ten inches apart from each other," Nick said while still demonstrating. "Ok, let's go!"

We all jumped up, crowding the doorway to get down the hall and outside of the double doors that led to the garden. Let's be honest, it was a competition, and we all wanted to find the buried treasure first.

I went directly to the locations that I marked with an X. I found the first one hidden under a chair cushion. I then went for the second X, and with a little help from my eyes, I found the second envelope.

I was onto the third X on my map, which was also identified by two other students. This one proved to be harder to find without using the dowsing rods, so I put my map in my back pocket and pointed the rods in the direction where I thought the envelope was hidden. "Please show me where the envelope is." I asked.

I stepped forward, but then the rods began to point in opposite directions. I quickly stepped back, turned a step to my right, and repeated the question. The rods did the same thing. I stepped back again, took a step to my left, and then repeated the question. The rods began to cross slowly, but only at the very tips; therefore, I took another step forward and watched as they crossed a little bit more. After one more step, they crossed completely. I looked down and saw a large potted plant below my hands. I looked inside the pot but didn't find anything. But when I looked again, I noticed that it was a pot inside of another pot. The envelope was at the bottom! I wanted to spike it down to the ground like a game-winning touchdown, but I didn't want to gloat.

The last two envelopes were found by the other students while I was searching for mine. We all had a great time outside working with the dowsing rods. It was also a beautiful evening, so it was a win all the way around.

There were many classes that Nick began with a remote-viewing exercise. He made copies of a map with the target location, folded them up, sealed them in individual envelopes, and wrote the longitude and latitude on the outside. When we came into class, we found an envelope waiting for us on the table in front of each chair.

"Pick up the envelope in front of you, read the longitude and latitude written on it. Write down any impressions that you get." Nick instructed. Some of the students began scribbling things down a mile a minute, but not me. "When you are done, hover your hand over the top of it, trace the number with your fingers, or write the number down on a separate piece of paper. See if you get any impressions from doing that." When everyone finished, he had us hold the envelope between the palms of our hands, close our eyes, and take a few deep breaths. We sat with our eyes closed and relaxed in our chairs. "Focus on the contents of the envelope. What do you see? Is it a city, a desert, a mall? What do you hear, Traffic, trains, birds, silence? What do you smell, taste, and feel? Is it hot or cold? Write it all down."

It was actually a little scary how much information we got from these exercises. There was one in particular that spurred me to draw the scene out on paper. It was a dry park in the desert with dead trees, a large boulder in the middle, and dirt everywhere. When I opened the envelope at the end of the exercise, I was astonished to see the resemblance.

Generally speaking, however, I suck at remote viewing. I was so bad that it became an inside joke among us regulars. It was my least favorite exercise because I never seemed to get it right.

Sometimes, Nick surprised us with a mystery guest. The exercise was usually held during the second half of class. He began the exercise by giving us tidbits of information about the person to direct our intuition at the target. For example, he might say the following: "A friend of mine named John Doe will be calling tonight. I want you to zero in on his name and write down any information you receive about him. It could be his health, his occupation, his relationship, his children, or his pets. When you are done, look around him and see where he is. At work? At home? The kitchen? The living room? Write down everything you see."

I always began these exercises by writing down the person's name several times and waiting to receive information. This helped me clear my mind and avoid guessing. It happens a lot because humans like to be right. In short, it was a way to remove my ego from the equation.

Still, there were times when I swore that the information didn't come *from* me; instead, it came *through* me, channeled from a divine source into my subconscious. But when the mystery guest revealed his or her information, and I saw that it didn't match what I wrote down, I knew there was a disconnection.

I was right about half the time with this exercise. I received information about the person's health, relationships, children, and work. But I rarely scored well in terms of what they were wearing or which room of the house they were in. I think these issues stemmed from my problems with remote viewing.

A few times, the mystery guest asked the class for assistance. For instance, in one class, a woman was concerned about her son. She asked Nick whether we could provide a group reading for her about him. She was recently divorced from her son's father, and that created a shift in her son's behavior. She was concerned because he was acting differently.

Nick began the exercise by sharing a photo of the boy. In the photo, he looked like a conservative kid, thirteen or fourteen years old. He wore round, gold-rimmed glasses and a dress shirt. As we passed the photo around the table, Nick said, "His name is Adam. Write down the name and take note of any information you receive about him."

We were not remote viewing Adam, because even though he was a minor, there were ethical considerations at play. Generally speaking, remote viewing should only be used with the consent from the person in question.

Because we were *reading* him, though, I went through my usual process of writing his name down several times. I then looked at his photo and asked my spirit guides for assistance. Almost immediately, I felt like I had a blanket over my head. It reminded me of the people in commercials who are sick and have large towels draped over their heads.

I also felt a very different personality than what I saw in the picture. The boy felt like a skateboarder who played video games and liked to be outside, which was the complete opposite impression that I got from the photo. Also, he seemed smart but sad. I sensed that he was a good kid. Interestingly, I could also smell garlic. It was so strong that I thought it was coming from another room in the Learning Light ... it wasn't.

And then I felt myself wanting to lift my hand and move it in a circle, as if I were stirring something in a large pot. It was the weirdest feeling. I could also taste spaghetti sauce, so I put it all together and surmised that the kid liked to cook or eat spaghetti.

While writing these things down, I couldn't get past the feeling of the draped blanket. I put my pencil down and shared my thoughts with the class: "I keep feeling this blanket over my head; you know, like in the commercials when someone is sick." No one got it. A few minutes later, as I pondered it some more, I finally figured it out. "I know what it is!" I said, as I snapped my fingers and pointed to my notes. "It's a hoodie! He wears a hoodie all the time!" A huge sigh of relief ran over me.

Nick arranged for us to call her during the second half of class. When she answered, Nick switched the phone to speaker mode before introducing the class members to her. "Thank you, Nick. And thanks to all of you for helping me out." She said, sounding concerned about her son.

"Okay, let's go one by one around the table. Let's ask one question at a time based on the information you received," Nick said. "Who wants to go first?" I wanted to go last so I could focus on the questions that hadn't been asked yet.

Patiently, I listened to the questions and answers and took note of anything similar that I picked up. I noticed that no one picked up on the hoodie, cooking, or skateboarding. I wondered whether I was completely wrong.

When it was my turn, I said, "He is a good kid and gets good grades. I don't see that changing. I don't believe that he is on drugs or depressed, but I feel sadness. It's like he is processing the changes in his life internally because he doesn't want to add to his parents troubles." She was relieved because she felt the exact same way. "Does he skateboard? I can see him carrying a skateboard around," I asked.

"Yes!" she said excitedly. "He loves to skateboard. He takes it with him everywhere we go!" I then moved on to the cooking: "I kept seeing him stirring something and smelled garlic. Does he cook or like eating spaghetti?" I could hear her laughing.

"Yes, he loves to cook. His favorite dish is spaghetti." We all laughed a bit because it wasn't every day that we ran into a young boy who enjoyed cooking. My son won't even make his own bologna sandwiches.

My last question was about the hoodie: "I kept feeling like I had a blanket over my head. Does your son wear a hoodie most of the time?" I asked tentatively.

"Yes, he does. It is blue, and he doesn't leave home without it. In fact, he keeps the hood up most of the time while he is wearing it. I guess that is his way of tuning everything out," she explained.

We had gone full circle from the emotional to the physical and back again. "He is a good kid," I said. She agreed.

There were a few more questions asked by the class after that. It turned out to be a really good reading for her and all of us.

Nick and I still keep in touch. Every now and then, he will invite me to participate as the mystery guest for his class. I like to shake things up by wearing something crazy. The last time, I wore a fluffy scarf that was pink and purple and looked like it came off the set of *Fraggle Rock*.

What I Learned in Class

- I am remote viewing challenged.
- I love playing with dowsing rods.
- It is super fun working with a pendulum to locate people or objects.
- Working with a mystery guest provides immediate feedback that helps me understand the difference between information that comes *from* me (guessing) vs. *through* me (channeling).
- A great instructor makes all the difference!

The Writer's Workshop Weekend with Cheryl Richardson, Reid Tracy, and Nancy Levin

There were three courses that I attended in 2012 while I continued my Thursday evening classes with Nick at the Learning Light. The first one was the writer's workshop weekend, held at the Doubletree Hilton in Santa Monica, California. The speakers were Cheryl Richardson, Reid Tracy, and Nancy Levin.

I am a bookworm who reads a lot of non-fiction about the metaphysical and supernatural aspects of the universe. The fiction I read often combines the supernatural with romance. I never aspired to be a writer, until one day I woke up and declared, "I want to write a book." The idea shocked me, and I had no idea where to start.

After searching through dozens of books on Amazon and comparing their reviews, I picked up *Writing Fiction for Dummies* by Randy Ingermanson and Peter Economy. It turned out to be an excellent book for a complete novice like myself. I was not an English major; in fact, I don't have a college degree. Hell, I barely made it through high school! My only advanced education came from the local community college. There, I studied math, psychology, Spanish, and dance. Math sucked, psychology was fun, Spanish was hard, and dance was awesome. Despite that lack of education, however, a little voice kept telling me to write. Therefore, I hit the Internet to see what I could find locally. When I found the writer's workshop weekend sponsored by Hay House, I knew what to do. It was just an hour drive into Los Angeles, and I only needed to stay one night at the Doubletree Hilton. I was in.

About six months before the workshop, I developed a skin disorder called melasma. When it develops during pregnancy, some people refer to it as the mask of pregnancy. Melasma presents as dark patches on the cheeks, upper lip, chin, and forehead. My doctor determined that mine developed as a result of taking oral contraceptives. But by the time I decided to discontinue taking the pill, it was too late. Essentially, the damage was already done.

The spots started off small. Initially, they were little, round, brown circles on my cheeks, but they continued to get larger and larger over time. Eventually, they appeared on my upper lip too. One morning, I woke up, looked in the mirror, and thought, *Wow, I look like my grandfather who used to dye his mustache and eyebrows black.* He reminded me of Groucho Marx. Anyway, it was awful. People literally stopped and stared at me when I went out in public.

One afternoon, I took my truck to the car wash. I was sitting outside under a large umbrella when a young couple came out. The woman kept staring at me. I was wearing sunglasses, but I could see her out of the corner of my eye. At one point, she was standing right in front of me and gawking, which made me very uncomfortable. *Stupid, nosey hag,* I thought. Fortunately, they called my number to claim my truck shortly thereafter. And that was the last time I went anywhere alone for months.

I hid inside our home all week. I only went out on the weekend with Kurt to a few places where we knew the bartenders. I kept my head down and avoided eye contact with everyone else. I became extremely depressed; I felt lonely and isolated even though it was self-induced. Because I worked from home, my condition didn't affect my job, but I was dying on the inside.

One day, I called my mom crying. "Mama, am I a bad person? Am I mean to people? What did I do to deserve this? I must have done something, right?" My mom assured me that I was a good person—I was a short-tempered person at times, but I was good in general. She reminded me to have faith that it would heal eventually. She was right, but it was hard because I have never been a patient person.

I knew there was no cure, and that made my depression worse. My self-esteem plummeted into nonexistence. Luckily, this was when I found the writer's workshop. I figured that it was close by, so if I couldn't handle it, I could turn around and come home. In the end, I signed up.

The drive was tricky because I had to keep my face out of the sun. The spots absorb sunlight and get darker, like a tan. To avoid that fate, I drove the whole way with one hand holding a folded piece of paper in front of my face. I thought about cutting little holes to see out of it, but I decided that that was really dangerous and would freak out the other drivers. I also tried driving with a bandana covering the lower half of my face, but I couldn't breathe well and went back to the other method.

I arrived in one piece that morning, checked into my hotel room, and went downstairs to the conference room for registration. Tables were set up in the back of the conference room, right inside the double doors. It was the first time I got to see Cheryl Richardson speak in person, which thrilled me because I loved her. She was the reason I wanted to attend the workshop. Sadly, that thrill shriveled up before the workshop began.

While I was standing at the table for registration, I noticed Cheryl standing behind the tables and looking toward the stage. Shortly after that, I watched her sit down in one of the chairs. I was pretty excited to be there, to be a writer, to get out of the house for a few days. At that moment, everything was good.

I was greeted by a woman with a warm smile and a positive attitude. After she signed me in, she handed me a writer's workshop workbook, a hardcover writing journal, and a pen. As I walked toward the seating area, I looked over at Cheryl. She was frowning as she looked me up and down. I immediately became self-conscious of my face, but I managed to greet her as I walked directly in front of her. She stared at me with a combined look of boredom and disgust before turning to speak to the woman next to her as if I didn't exist. *What was that all about? I was standing right in front of her, she couldn't have missed me.*

Puzzled by her actions, I walked into the huge conference room. There were a couple hundred chairs set up, and they were laid out in three sections: one set of rows down the middle, and one set against each wall. There were two main aisles leading up to the large stage in the front of the room. I sat in an aisle seat about halfway up while going over what happened in my head. *That was so freaking weird.*

The seats were filling up fast. When most of them were full, the workshop began. Reid Tracy was the key facilitator. I became a fan of his after the workshop. There were introductions, an overview of the schedule, and a video with Wayne Dyer that was very good.

Over the next day and a half, the keynote speakers took the stage to tell their stories. They shared the ups and downs of writing a book and the journey that led them to being published writers. The first day featured Nancy and Reid. They were very inspirational, but I wondered when the workshop portion of class would start? That question continued to plague me.

I managed to make it through the first day with no issues. I ate lunch with a group of students at a large table in the hotel. It went well; I didn't get any weird looks about my spots. I had dinner at the bar that evening where I met a handful of students from out of town. They were a riot, and they couldn't stop laughing about their journey to the conference, their books, their publishers, etc. It was informative and entertaining. After a few glasses Miller Lite, I said my good-byes and went back to my room. It was obvious that I was in over my head. I needed more than a weekend workshop of people telling me their stories to get me going.

The next morning started off smoothly. I figured we would finally learn about writing that day. Wrong. Instead, we moved into the marketing portion of the class. Because I was far from that point, I just listened and took notes. Unfortunately, my diligent note-taking was interrupted by a *click, click, click*. The noise was really distracting, and it made it hard to hear what others were saying on stage. I looked around until I found the source: a woman in the middle section typing on her iPad's keyboard with her fingernails. She was being rude—not just to the speaker, but also to all of us who paid a lot of cash to be there. Several of the students around her stared in her direction, but she didn't get the hint or didn't care. A few people actually got up and moved. Luckily, a break was announced at that point.

As I stood in line for the restroom, I noticed that the woman standing in front of me was one of the people sitting next to the fingernail typist. "The typing is really annoying, right?" I asked. She started to answer while turning around to look at me, but she stopped mid-sentence when she saw my upper lip. She couldn't stop staring. I suppose that, because she was much shorter than I am, my spots were directly in her line of sight. I'm sure the florescent lighting didn't help either. She never finished her sentence; instead, she just turned back around slowly. I wanted to cry and run, but I did neither; I just stood there looking down at my shoes and waiting for my turn. The situation broke my heart.

After the break, the focus shifted to publishing and promoting books. People were given the opportunity to ask questions. They lined up in one of the aisles and waited for the chance to use the microphone that stood in front of the stage. Because I didn't have a manuscript ready or a partly written book, I didn't have any questions. And, it became obvious that they weren't going to teach us how to write. I was disappointed.

What I figured out was that it wasn't a workshop about *learning* how to write; rather, it was a workshop geared toward *inspiring* us to write. The class was designed to teach us how to get published, self-publish, or market our books. After listening to a few of the questions, I packed up my things and left a few hours early.

Cheryl turned out to be a great speaker, but it was too late: my first impression was etched into my memory. I went home that evening and removed my "like" from her Facebook page.

What I Learned in Class

- The word *workshop* doesn't necessarily mean an event is an actual workshop.
- Avoid interacting with keynote speakers before the event.
- Balboa Press is awesome!

Advanced Numerology with Alison Baughman

A few months after the writer's workshop, I took a one-day advanced numerology (distance learning) class with Alison Baughman. I already knew Alison from getting a yearly numerology reading from her. She was a no-nonsense kind of gal, and I loved that.

The class materials were e-mailed to us prior to the start date. This allowed us to become familiar with the terms and definitions. She also included our personal numerology chart for the year, along with the charts of our immediate family members if we requested them, which I did.

There were about twelve of us on the call that day. Alison began with introductions, an overview of the course, and the history of numerology. After allowing time for questions, she walked us through the ins and outs of our charts. This was not an easy task—numerology is no place for wusses.

We began by learning the methodology through which we could identify various core numbers in our charts—the life path, birthday, expression, heart's desire, and personality numbers. Next, she taught us the high-level meanings of each number so we could understand those parts of ourselves. We also reviewed them within the charts of our family members to understand how the interaction between the different numbers (and within the different relationships) played out. I didn't have to stretch anything to make it fit. It was obvious when I looked at the big picture.

Like my course in astrology, it was very revealing and complex. It is its own language with many variables, such as the date you were born, the letters in your name at birth, your home address, your business address, etc. You can also use numerology to find a new home or place of business based on the address.

We spent a lot of time working through the comparison of our charts with our family members and significant others. The majority of the questions revolved around relationships.

"Alison, I am a seven life path and Kurt is a four. Based on the information we are learning, I'm more spiritual, a seeker. Kurt is a more practical, business-oriented person. Are we a mismatch?" I asked. Alison went through each of our charts methodically, pointing out the areas where balance was required to avoid beating the crap out of each other.

The greatest part of the class was interacting with Alison. It was as interactive as we wanted it to be, and we could stop and ask questions whenever we liked.

It was no surprise that, by the end of the class, everyone was asking when she was going to write a book. The great news is that she took some time off of her very busy schedule and wrote one in 2013: *Speaking to Your Soul Through Numerology*. I bought it and began working with it as soon as it came out.

At the time of this writing, I am in a six essence this year (at age 49). I was in an eight essence for the last six years. The six essence focuses on affairs of the home, family, children, and loved ones. The 15/6 essence emphasizes problems with the opposite sex. Knowing this, I will take extra caution to avoid fighting with Kurt. *Wink!*

What I Learned in Class

- Numerology opens you up to a whole new way of looking at numbers.
- Numerology offers some very valuable insight about yourself and others.
- A yearly reading is a must!

Spoon Bending PK Party
with JacQuaeline

The last class I took in 2012 was a one-day course in spoon bending by JacQuaeline of Intuition Power. It was held on a Saturday afternoon in June at the Learning Light Foundation.

I had heard of the class, but knew very little about what it entailed. I couldn't imagine spending five hours just trying to bend spoons. But if there was a way to bend metal with my mind, I wanted to know how. You never know when a skill like that could come in handy.

I showed up to class bright-eyed and bushy-tailed. Every part of me was excited to be there. I had a Diet Coke in my hand and a water bottle in my bag. I was ready to go.

We were in the large lecture hall on the main floor that had vaulted ceilings and stained glass windows. The chairs were set up in a large circle toward the front of the room. A long reception table was set up between the circle of chairs and the stage, and it had all kinds of bent spoons and forks on it. It also had pamphlets and boxes of new forks sealed in plastic bags.

There were approximately twenty-five of us in the class, and there was a buzz in the air. We were like little kids waiting in line to enter Disneyland. We were all chatting with each other, trying to contain our enthusiasm.

JacQuaeline began with a short introduction about herself and her history of bending spoons and forks. While she was talking, she handed us several of the bent utensils from the table to pass around. We were in awe. Several of the students tried to bend them some more thinking that the metal was soft, but they had no success. Right at that time, she gave an explanation about the torque, weight, and strength necessary to bend a spoon at the bowl. The physics were fascinating.

Right about then, doubt started to creep in. The truth is, we generally don't think much about our silverware. The forks, spoons, and knives are just tools we use to get food into our mouths. So until we actually held some of the ones that were already bent, we felt totally capable. But when we held them and tried to bend them, we came to the realization that it was not about being strong. We had to learn the Jedi mind trick. Were we worthy?

JacQuaeline was a cool character. When I looked at her, I saw an attractive woman who seemed normal. But she also reminded me of an instructor for driver's education class. She knew she had to keep our attention long enough to teach us the basics, in order for us to get behind the wheel at the end of class. But all we cared about was getting behind the wheel at the end of class. Fortunately, she kept us under control with her mind. She was Yoda.

After a short question-and-answer session, JacQuaeline went over to the table and brought back several bags of unbent forks and began emptying them onto the carpet in the middle of the circle. "Okay, everyone, we are going to begin with forks," she said as she continued what she was doing with the help of one of the students. "You are going to hold the fork in front of you by the handle, prongs facing up," she explained while picking up a new fork from the pile and holding it out in front of her. "And then, with intention, you are going to tell your fork to bend," she said as she looked straight at the prongs. She then said, "Bend, bend, *bend!*" We all waited to see it move.

And then, slowly, she began to bend the fork, first at the neck, and then at the prongs. Once again, we were all in awe. After that, she turned to us and said, "Now it is your turn. Everyone, come over and pick out seven forks from the pile. Take them back to your seat with you, but don't begin yet. We are going to wait until everyone is ready." We all rushed the pile like someone had cracked open a piñata filled with hundred dollar bills. I took my time selecting each fork that looked like it wanted to work with me. I know that sounds crazy because they all looked exactly the same, but that's how I felt.

We all sat with our forks in hand until everyone returned to their seats, which seemed like two days went by. And then JacQuaeline, who has a positive energy that pulls you to her like a magnet, finally spoke: "Pick one fork. Place the rest of them on the floor underneath your chair, or beside you and out of the way. And then you can begin." *Woohoo!*

I grabbed my fork, dumped the rest on the ground underneath my chair, took a deep breath, held the fork in front of me, and said to myself, *You are so beautiful! Thank you for allowing me to work with you.* And then I told it to bend ... *bend!* I have to admit that I felt like an evil bitch for yelling at the poor fork that did nothing wrong. At least when I yell at Kurt and the kids, they deserve it. But this poor fork didn't.

It took me a few laughs with the class to get over the strangeness of the situation and really mean what I was saying. And that is when I felt the heat in my hand start to rise. I also felt the fork *shift*, as if it were relaxing. It felt like holding a fussy child who eventually stops crying and falls asleep on your chest. The fork actually relaxed, as I held onto it with both hands to see whether I could bend it. I could. I bent it at the neck and twisted it into a spiral. When I was in the process of bending the prongs, it became stiff again. *Weird,* I thought.

When many students started having success with the first fork, JacQuaeline encouraged us to move on to the second and third forks. She walked around the room providing assistance. Some of the students were standing up instead of sitting in their chair to get the energy flowing. Others were walking around the room begging their fork to bend. We were all a sight to see, I'm sure.

After a short break, we moved on to spoons. JacQuaeline reminded us how much more difficult it was to bend a spoon at the bowl. She held up several examples of the ones that were sitting on the table. As she was talking, she grabbed a bunch of new ones and walked around the circle. She allowed us to pick one out for the exercise. There were modern-looking ones, antique ones, and other styles. "Remember that emotion helps when bending a spoon. Try thinking about a sad moment in your life, focus on it while holding the spoon," she said. It was a lot harder than it sounds.

After each person picked out a spoon, she told us to begin. *Here I go again. Bend ... bend!* I said the words internally with gusto, but nothing happened. I did it again. Nothing. And then, finally, I began to feel the heat rising in my hand. The spoon relaxed a little, but I was only able to bend the neck a tiny bit. It was strange. I felt disappointed until I looked around to see all the other students having the same luck.

There were only two people who successfully bent their spoon at the bowl. One was a paranormal investigator named Chris. He was sitting toward the front of the room in a big, comfy chair. The look on his face when he bent the bowl of the spoon was priceless. When he looked up, I was staring straight at him. He held out his hand with the spoon sitting on top of it as if to say, "Check this out! I did it!" I couldn't stop smiling as I nodded in response and gave him a thumbs up.

I walked over to him and said, "That was awesome! How did you do it? How did it feel?" Everyone else quieted down to hear his response. "I don't know. JacQuaeline said to think of a sad moment, so I did. And then I felt the spoon get warm. And then it just folded in my hand." He replied. He was fanning himself with a piece of paper as he spoke because he was sweating pretty intensely. Apparently, the process had raised his body temperature a lot. *Interesting.*

The rest of the students were still desperately trying to bend their spoons, but JacQuaeline announced that we were moving on to the next exercise. "Please put your spoons away in a safe place with your forks and take out a few pennies, dimes, nickels, or quarters. If you don't have any loose change, ask to borrow some from one of the other students." I dug out some spare change, one of each coin.

JacQuaeline then began the demonstration using a penny. She walked over to the wall, placed the penny flat on it, and then, while holding it in place with her index finger, she said, "Stay … *stay!*" After that, she stepped backward and pulled her index finger off of the penny slowly. It stuck to the wall. *It is just stuck to the paint on the wall, right?* As if she were reading my thoughts, she said, "If you think that the penny is just stuck to the paint, try it on another surface like the wood door." After she spoke, I realized that the paint on the walls was not shiny; it was flat, old, and dry. I don't think the paint could have caused it to stick if it tried.

Off we went, telling our pocket change to stick to the walls. I couldn't help laughing through the entire process. We were nuts. I was sure of it as I took my penny, held it against the wall, and told it to stay. It was very subtle, but I could feel the energetic disconnect at the tip of my finger. And then it felt like it was letting go. When I took my finger off of it, it stuck! *Holy crap! It worked!* I went around the room with the rest of my crazy peers trying the maneuver on different surfaces using different coins. I had the best luck with pennies and dimes. Nickels were okay, quarters struck out.

Unfortunately, I can't remember the exact words we used to ask the coin to release itself from the wall, but I think we said, "Let go." Before saying those words, the coins remained in place.

After another short break, we began our last exercise for the day. JacQuaeline provided an overview of the process for growing a bean sprout in our hands, allowing a few minutes for questions before we got started. "Please hold out one of your hands," she stated as she walked around the circle. "I am going to place a bean in it for you to work with." They looked moist, and some of them had begun to sprout.

When I put out my hand, she placed a bean that was split on one side into it. I cupped my other hand over it, closed my eyes, took a deep breath, and asked it to grow. *Grow, little bean ... grow.* I kept my eyes closed until I felt my hands start to heat up. When I peeked inside my hands, I noticed that nothing had changed. I cleared my mind, concentrating the energy into my hands while I continued to ask my little bean to grow. But nothing happened.

I continued to cup it in my hands while I chatted away with some of the students sitting next to me who were also taking the class for the first time. We laughed with each other about the exercises, bending our forks, not being able to bend our spoons, and sticking coins to the wall. It had been a fun-filled day, totally worth the price of tuition.

When JacQuaeline came around to collect the beans, mine had grown a little leaf! It had sprouted in my hand while I was talking to my peers. I wanted to cry it was so cute! In fact, I deemed it the cutest little bean sprout ever.

When I got home that evening, I shared the events with Kurt and the kids. They looked my forks over with the same look that I had at the beginning of class. Eventually, I put the forks away in a basket by my desk, but I kept the spoon sitting out by my monitor. It was a constant reminder of unfinished business.

And then, one lazy Saturday afternoon about six months later, I was watching one of the Harry Potter movies on TV with Travis. He was sitting at the kitchen table while I sat on the couch. The heroine, Hermione Granger, had just used her wand to do something spectacular. Being a lover of all things magic, especially magic wands, I stood up and said, "That's it! I can do this! I am going to bend that spoon!" I walked over to my desk, held the spoon in my hand, and said, "Bend! Be—" But before I was able to get the second request out, it started to relax. I took it in both hands and bent the handle as if it were paper. After that, I placed it in the palm of my hand and closed my hand gently. The bowl bent in half. It felt like a rose petal, soft and smooth. "Oh my God! Oh my God!" I said while freaking out. I looked up at Travis. He had a look of complete disbelief on his face. But then, just as quickly as it turned to butter, it became as solid as a rock again.

Travis and I were hooting and hollering. He walked over to take it out of my hand. "It's hot," he said. "Yeah. Crazy, huh? It is all the energy exchanged between us," I replied, still in absolute shock.

My hands were lit up, but so was my third chakra, which is located in the solar plexus. I could feel the heat radiating in a giant circle from just below my chin, down to the top of my thighs. The energy had weight to it to, like a thick, invisible air pillow. I was also sweating as if I had just been sprinting, but my heart was calm. That was, without a doubt, the coolest thing I had done so far, and I had a witness to prove it!

What I Learned in Class

- Psychokinesis (PK) is real. Imagine the possibilities.
- I can bend a spoon and fork using my mind and energy.
- We are capable of growing plants from seeds in our hands.
- The X-Men are definitely real.

Did You Say Virginia? But I Have Never Been There Before!

At the end of 2012, Kurt, Travis, and I took a trip to Washington, D.C., to visit my daughter, Sydney, for Thanksgiving. It was her second year with the Navy, and she had just been stationed at Joint Base Anacostia-Bolling (JBAB). When we returned home, Kurt had a voicemail from a senior leader at the financial institution where he worked. They had an opening that he thought Kurt would be interested in. This was good news because it was a position Kurt wanted, but it was bad news because the position was located in McLean, Virginia. At least *I* thought that was bad news.

When he told me, I couldn't believe what I was hearing. "I really want this opportunity, Rena. It would be a great step," Kurt said. I knew he was right, that it would be good for him. *But what about me?* I thought.

Because I was fortunate enough to work from home, I knew I didn't have that argument. And because we lived in an overpriced, three-bedroom apartment in one of the most expensive areas in Orange County, I didn't have that argument either. We didn't own a house to sell, so I struck out there too. It really came down to Travis, who grew up in California and had all his friends there. He had just turned fourteen a few months earlier.

Kurt returned the gentleman's call first thing the next morning, and he was on a flight to northern Virginia for an interview two days later. I was pissed. After that, there was a second interview. I was in denial. And then they made him an offer in December. I tried to talk him out of it, but it didn't work. They wanted him to start on the first of the year, and I knew he was leaving.

As Kurt and Travis flew back to Virginia to look at schools, I stayed behind to watch the dog and start packing.

I couldn't believe Travis was onboard. He loved California and was never home because he was outside playing baseball or riding his skateboard with his friends. How the hell would he survive the winters? I came to the conclusion that Kurt must have bribed him with a new car when he got his license.

Two weeks after the offer was made, we were packed up and on our way to Virginia. Kurt, Travis, Stitch, and I drove across the country in Kurt's truck, pulling a small U-Haul in the middle of winter. Worst. Holiday. Season. Ever.

Even though I didn't have any family in California, it was a short drive to my family in Arizona. And even though I rarely spent any time with my family in Arizona, I knew they were close by. Everything was changing, and I felt like it was completely out of my control. I could stay, but without my kids, it would be meaningless. So I went along for the ride. Sometimes in life we do that.

We pulled up to the Marriott in Fairfax, Virginia, about forty-five minutes before midnight on New Year's Eve. Kurt and Travis went to find food and beer. I laid in bed crying. I had nothing to celebrate; I hated everyone but the dog.

To make this long, miserable story short, 2013 started with us living in a crappy, three–bedroom, bottom floor apartment that reeked like cigarette smoke. After that, we moved into a very nice condo for two years. Unfortunately, it smelled like garlic most of the time due to our neighbor's cooking. I *hate* the smell of garlic. We also had to deal with the thumping sound system of the idiots next door.

Now we live in a three-bedroom town home with a two-car garage. I throw that last bit in because I haven't had a garage since

I left my house in Arizona. It is such a gift to have a parking spot instead of circling a parking lot looking for an open space every time I return home. So far we are happy, but that could be all the Miller Lite talking.

The Gateway Voyage at the Monroe Institute

It was now summer, and I hadn't attended any classes since our move to Virginia. It was time to get out and meet new people. Not knowing quite what to expect, I got online to search for something in the area. And that's when a kind of synchronicity worked its magic.

The only mediumship class I found was on Meetup.com, which seemed a little sketchy, mostly because I was not familiar with it and it felt a little like Internet dating. After that short search, I gave up and turned on the TV. Coincidentally, there was a paranormal documentary on the History Channel about the lifeline program at the Monroe Institute in Faber, Virginia. I grabbed my atlas and looked it up online. The institute was only a few hours away. I could drive there, no problem!

As I read through the information online, I found out that, in order to attend the lifeline program, you had to take a prerequisite course called the gateway voyage. Not all the programs had prerequisites, but this one did. I looked at the dates that were listed for upcoming classes. There was one with space available at the end of July. I knew we had nothing going on, so I gave them a call and registered for the class.

About a week later, I received a package in the mail from the Monroe Institute. It was a welcome packet with a brochure and several handouts. They also included a CD of the Hemi-Sync binaural-beat technology that we would be working with. One of the handouts gave us a list of what to bring and what to leave at home. This made it easy to pack.

The drive over was beautiful. Winter was long gone, everything was in full bloom, and it was green everywhere I looked. It rained off and on, which made it a little hard to see at times. But all in all, it was a nice drive.

After making great time, I arrived with some to spare before registration on Saturday. I was greeted by a sweetheart of a woman who checked my name off of the list and walked me to my room. "You will be the only one in your room for this class," she said. "Really? That's great!" I replied. She agreed.

The room's onsite are semi-private accommodations. You can request that you are the only one in your room, but if the class is full, you will have a roommate. This is pretty standard for programs that have accommodations on-site.

All the bathrooms were shared as well. There were a few half baths, and the rest were full bathrooms with showers. This was weird because we saw each other walking around in bathrobes, which was kind of uncomfortable because we were total strangers. It was like summer learning camp for adults. The funny thing is, by the end of the week, no one cared anymore.

The beds were not ordinary beds. They were completely enclosed except for a portion of the front side that allowed you to get in and out. There was a heavy black curtain that you used to block out all the light once you were inside. They called them bed chambers or CHEC (Controlled Holistic Environmental Chamber) units.

Inside the bed chamber was a very comfortable mattress, a few pillows, a light that was attached to the wall, a small speaker, a set of large headphones, a volume control for the speaker and headphones, and a red indicator light with a notification switch. This is where we spent a good portion of our class time during the day for the exercises that used the Hemi-Sync audio guidance technology.

After I put my things away in my room, I went downstairs for the meet and greet. They served appetizers, water, coffee, and tea. We were all asked to avoid alcohol and caffeine as much as possible during our stay. This information was included in the welcome package that was sent to us, so I brought a couple of six packs of caffeine-free Diet Coke with me. I figured, if the other students could drink coffee, I should be able to drink my soda. There was plenty of filtered water provided throughout the week as well. We went through gallons of it per day between the exercises and the heat outside.

During the meet and greet, we met our two instructors, Scott and Patty. They held individual, one-on-one sessions with each student during that first evening. Mine was with Patty, and it went something like this:

> **Patty**: "What are your expectations for the class?"
> **Me**: "To learn something new."
> **Patty**: "Have you ever had an out-of-body experience?"
> **Me**: "No." (At least not the way they explained it.[3])

The chance to have an out-of-body experience (OBE) was the main reason most of the students were there. But that wasn't the reason I was there. I just viewed the class as the prerequisite to the one I really wanted to take, so I didn't have any questions for Patty or any experiences to share.

When the one-on-one sessions were finished, we went to an adjacent building that had a conference room with tables, chairs, and a small stage. We watched a video about the Monroe Institute founder, Robert (Bob) Monroe, his family, and the Hemi-Sync technology. It was very informative. After that, they took all of our

---

[3] See Appendix: My out-of-Body Experience.

watches and placed them in a wooden box to keep us from worrying about the time. Of course, it wasn't the seventies anymore, and we all used our cell phones to keep track of time now—watches were just jewelry. Still, we went along with it.

We were also asked to limit our communication with the outside world in order to stay focused on the program. There were no TVs or radios; instead, we were encouraged to take walks, swim in the lake, or read a book. This helped us remain disconnected electronically. I took a few books and my Kindle.

Next, we had to interview the person next to us. We used that information to introduce that person to the class. It was odd, uncomfortable, and a little annoying. *Exactly how is this helping me with my out-of-body experience?*

When the introductions were finished, we were done for the night. We went back to the main building to get ready for bed. Some of the students stayed up in the living room talking. Most of us were tired and headed straight for our rooms.

Sleep sounds were piped into our bed chamber each night at the same time. If we wanted to listen, we had to put on the headphones so we didn't interrupt our roommates. After taking off my makeup and brushing my teeth in a shared bathroom, I went to sleep, eager to get started the next morning.

I woke up to music. It was used to let us know that there was one hour before breakfast would be ready. Once I figured that out, I set my cell phone alarm thirty minutes earlier to give me time to shower. Yes, that was definitely cheating.

Breakfast was buffet style. I had the added luxury of drinking my caffeine-free Diet Coke. After breakfast, we met in the "Fox Den." It was a large room with wall-to-wall wood paneling and ivory carpet. There was a large, champagne-colored area rug in the middle with the Monroe Institute logo on it. It was cozy with several love seat-sized sofas along two of the walls and chairs shaped like an *L* that sat directly on the floor with no legs. Two easels stood at the front of the room for the instructors to use during lectures.

There was also a stack of big pillows. This space quickly became my favorite room on campus.

We created a large half circle with the chairs facing the front. I managed to sit in the same spot throughout the week. Before our first exercise, Patty and Scott provided an overview of how the Hemi-Sync audio technology worked. It was not a short explanation.

There were also possible side effects. We could have an OBE if we wanted to, or we could "click-out," which was the term used for lost time. In addition, we could experience dizziness or get headaches. It was important that we understood that we were in charge of ourselves; no one was controlling us. In short, we could stop participating in an exercise at any time.

Patty and Scott shared stories of their own experiences over the years, and they also shared the experiences of other people with whom they went to class. I found them funny and fascinating at the same time. They explained that it was very important to write each experience in our journal immediately after each exercise ended. To do this, we were provided with a medium-sized notebook and a pen.

"It is also very important to stay hydrated. Please make sure that you keep a bottle of water with you at all times throughout the week," Patty explained. This information was also included in our welcome kit so we could bring a refillable bottle from home.

"If you need to use the restroom, please do so before we begin. We want to avoid people getting up during the exercise, which can disrupt the other students," Scott said. "I will begin piping music through the headphones while everyone gets settled into their units. Once you are ready with headphones on, lights off, and curtains closed, turn your red indicator light off by flipping the switch next to it. That will let me know in the control room that your unit is ready. We cannot begin until everyone's indicator light is off." We all nodded to show we understood. "Before we begin, do you have any questions?" The room was silent. "Okay, everyone to their rooms!" Scott said. He was a funny guy who wore themed socks every day.

I could hear people running around upstairs, and the sounds of doors opening and closing as the students got ready. I jumped into my unit, shut the curtain, grabbed my headphones, and flipped the indicator light off.

As soon as I put my headphones on, I could hear Scott's voice: "Hello, everyone, this is some easy listening music to help you relax before we get started. We are still waiting on units seven and ten to turn off their indicator lights." It was nice of them to avoid calling us out by name. And then I heard, "Okay, we have an all-clear." Scott's voice was nice and mellow as the Hemi-Sync began.

I completely relaxed, sinking deeper and deeper into my mattress as I listened to the techno-groovy sounds of the Hemi-Sync. My arms, legs, and head became lighter and lighter until I couldn't feel them anymore. I thought I was floating somewhere between awake and asleep until I heard Scott's voice again. Like a guided meditation, we were brought back out of the semiconscious state gently. Scott's voice was like a cool jazz radio DJ guiding us through the next steps.

"As you begin to wake up, remember to reach up and turn your red indicator light back on." There was a short pause with background music before he continued: "Good, good. Remember to bring your water bottles and journal with you downstairs for group share." I opened my curtain, switched my socks from the ones I wore in bed, grabbed my things, and went straight downstairs.

Because I was one of the first students in the Fox Den, I started journaling my experience immediately. It was not a life-changing experience … it was like a very deep, relaxing sleep.

Scott and Patty looked wide awake, but the rest of us were drinking water, trying to keep our eyes open. "Let's take some time to share our experiences with the group. This is not mandatory. Is there anyone who would like to go first?" Scott asked. A few of the students raised their hands. As they were talking, the rest of us were listening or journaling. I was doing a little of both.

In the beginning, many of the experiences were the same. This changed throughout the week as we progressed into the deeper levels of Hemi-Sync. We went back to our units for another exercise and group share before lunch. Here are my journal entries:

First Exercise

Extremely relaxed. Felt completely separate from my physical body. Toward the end, I found myself thinking about everyday things right before Bob's voice (in the Hemi-Sync) started counting down to wake up.

Second Exercise

I remember feeling the sensation of lifting up out of my body when coming back to C1 (a level of Hemi-Sync), and then I went back out again. I actually felt like I was going to levitate.

Before we left the Fox Den for lunch, we stood up in a circle and held hands for "resonate tuning." I loved this part. It is more commonly known as an *om* (a type of humming sound). Bob called it *resonate tuning* so that it was not linked to any particular dogma. I swear there were times that I thought I was going to float up off the ground from the vibration we created. It was that powerful.

Although I didn't actually time it, lunch was over two hours long. This was fine the first day, but beyond that, it became a real challenge for me. The food was good, served buffet style like breakfast, but after I ate, I was bored out of my mind. I didn't spend much time outside, because it was hot and humid. So I either went back to my room to disconnect or wandered around aimlessly. I wanted to grab one of the outside chairs and sit in the grass, but I was terrified of the giant, flesh-eating ticks that we were warned about. Who wanted to go home with Lyme disease?

After lunch, we continued our Hemi-Sync exercises twice more. Here are my journal entries:

Third Exercise (Dolphin Energy)

I remember feeling extremely cold. My feet and body became like ice, and I started shivering. I fell asleep. I stretched the bars and changed the color, but fell asleep without seeing the dolphins. Possible click-out. Not sleep, not awake, possible download from higher self. This could be healing.

Fourth Exercise (Discovering Life Purpose; How to Heal My Melasma)

Tom was my dolphin. He told me not to worry, that all the healing was done. I sat down with Doreen Virtue and she explained that my melasma would continue to heal as my self-confidence rose. As I continued to go back into the world and stop making excuses, it would continue to heal. It is beyond me now. It is in my past with issues of self-confidence. I no longer have them, so I no longer have melasma.

My soul purpose is to be happy and to live, love, and heal. My energy will help those I come in contact with.

I saw myself as electric blue energy. I was told I was one of them, a crystal energy being. That is why I get headaches when I come in contact with some crystals. I am them, they are me!

After the last exercise, I was ready to give my brain a rest. When we were done with group share, we stood in a circle for resonate tuning, and then we took a break for dinner.

Not long after we ate, we went to the building with the conference room across the lawn for our evening group activity. These included guest speakers. My favorite was with a remote-viewing expert, Joseph McMoneagle. He is the author of *Mind Trek* and *The Ultimate Time Machine.* Joseph was a researcher and remote viewer for the top secret army project called Stargate for more than seventeen years.

We didn't participate in a remote-viewing exercise; instead, we learned about the process through his experiences that began earlier in life. Because I was terrible at remote viewing, I listened to every single thing he said and tried to figure out what my issue was. I've come to the conclusion that it's just not going to be one of my strengths. Ever.

This was our routine for the week: Hemi-Sync exercises and discussions (about auras, etheric energy bodies, etc.) during the day and group activities in the conference room at night.

It wasn't until the end of the second day that I began to have a few experiences. The first was a loss of time, a click-out. We were coming out of our last Hemi-Sync exercise for the day. I heard Scott's familiar voice come over the headphones: "wakie wakie, it's time to get up. Don't forget to turn your indicator light back on and to grab your journal and bottle of water. See you in a few minutes." *Wow, I feel really tired. My head is totally pounding.*

I switched my socks, grabbed my things, and went directly downstairs. By this time, it was routine. But when I opened the door to my room, the floor was empty. No one was walking around, there were no sounds of doors opening or students taking a quick break in the bathroom. *Where is everyone? Did I just imagine Scott talking?* I honestly didn't know. Because I was always one of the first people downstairs, I figured I must have moved through my routine with lighting speed, so I kept walking down the stairs.

When I came around the corner, I couldn't believe what I saw. The room was full, and I was the only one missing. Slowly, I walked over to my spot and sat down, all the while looking around the room in disbelief. My facial expression must have said it all, because Scott looked at me with a huge smile and said, "Rena, are you okay? Is everything all right?" I replied, "No. How late am I? I don't understand. I came down just like I always do. How could I be late?"

"I think you just experienced a click-out, that loss of time we talked about. We have been down here for at least ten minutes," he explained. My jaw dropped, but no sound came out. I just sat there staring while trying to process what he said. There had to be a logical explanation, but no matter how many times I went through it in my mind, I never figured out how I lost almost fifteen minutes of time.

I didn't know whether to feel good or bad about the experience. On one side, I didn't age for fifteen minutes, but on the other side, I could have done something constructive with that fifteen minutes, like go to the restroom. I'm still in a quandary about it.

The second experience occurred the next day during our first morning exercise. I was lying in my bed chamber stoned on Hemi-Sync when I felt my hand chakras activate. I was on my back with my hands down by my sides, palms up, when I felt the sensation of a gyroscope spinning in both of my hands. The sensation had weight to it. It was so intense that I woke up out of the meditative state that I was in.

Slowly, I opened my eyes and looked at my hands to see whether there was anything there, but they looked perfectly normal. *What the hell is happening now?* This went on for a little less than half of the exercise. I couldn't relax, so I just laid there with my eyes open until I heard Scott's voice come over the headphones.

I couldn't wait to share my story with everyone. As soon as Scott said, "Did anyone have an experience they want to share?" I raised my hand. "Rena, how are you today?" Scott asked. "Good! I just had something really cool happen! A little more than halfway through the exercise, while I was lying on my back with my hands to my sides, palms up, I felt the chakras in my hands turn on!" Dead silence. *Why aren't these people saying anything? Don't they know what chakras are?*

In that moment, I forgot that this was not one of my psychic, mediumship, or healing classes. The class was not designed to align with any aspect of a particular belief system, and that included spirituality. This class was geared toward OBEs, which meant that the majority of the students had no idea what I was talking about. One didn't need to study metaphysics or be a spiritualist to be interested in or to have an OBE.

It was a total letdown. But I knew that Scott and Patty knew what chakras were. "Wow, that is really interesting," Patty said. *Was it? Was it really that interesting? Because you seem freaking calm!*

The discussion of chakras was kept at a very high level for the people who asked about them. And then we moved on to the next student's experience. Here is my journal entry:

> Focus 15: A man in a robe was there to meet me. His name was Tom, but he said I could call him Aristotle. The background was jewel-tone blue. We walked up a path like in Greece. He had white hair and beard. We went into the tower and looked over the city. He said my outfit was interesting. I asked whether it should be more feminine? He said, "Just nicer." He said I needed to forget trying to impress anyone and to focus on my abilities. There was the rub. I wanted to help, but I was afraid of failing.

- I woke up to my hand chakras spinning.
- I was told we all came from Africa, but people kept stealing the harvest, and that caused the initial problem.
- What was my focus on 15? To expand.
- At one point, I was putting myself through a table I was lying on. I then came out of it.
- I flew around Jupiter! It was very blue. I knew it was Jupiter. It was all about knowledge!
- I remember letting many masks fly off my face. This happened until my glowing, shining light of a face was left.

It was a truly awesome experience. Since that exercise, I can still feel the spinning sensation when I use my hands for healing.

By the last Hemi-Sync exercise of the week, I was fried. "No more!" my brain yelled. The rest of me concurred. I was ready to go home, eat food that wasn't good for me, and drink beer.

Those were the highlights of my time spent at the Monroe Institute. During our last evening together, the instructors surprised us with several ice chests full of various brands of soda to celebrate. It was awesome! It wasn't alcohol, but you wouldn't have known the difference by the way we drank it down while sharing stories about our time together and life in general.

What I Learned in Class

- The use of Hemi-Sync for meditation is a definite plus.
- Chakras are real.
- I don't like sharing showers with a dozen other people.
- Seeing men in short robes is creepy.
- I like having a private room.
- I want to attend the mc squared program in the future!

Mediumship Development Circle and PsyChicks with Sheila Cash

About six months after my week at the Monroe Institute, I found myself looking for a mediumship class again. It was my calling; I loved and missed working with spirit. I was hell-bent on finding a circle close by, so I went back to searching online and kept coming back to the posting on Meetup.com, which still seemed a little sketchy. But after reading the description, I noticed that it was very close.

The group was called the development of universal perception—evolving consciousness. *Okay, that sounds straightforward enough.* Within the group was a list of recent and upcoming events. One of them was an in-person development circle. *Yay!* There was also a weekly psychic development tele-class on Sunday evenings. The actual address wasn't provided, but the website noted that it was near Fair Oaks Mall in Fairfax, Virginia. That was less than two miles from where we lived.

The picture of the host, which could have been faked, was very pretty. I didn't get a creepy vibe at all. It was twenty-five dollars, and we could pay using PayPal. I wasn't sure what that was, but it seemed like a really good price for a two-hour session. So I went to the one person I knew who could demystify the whole PayPal and Meetup.com thing: Kurt.

"Hey, babe, I found this class on Meetup.com. It is a development circle over by the mall." I looked at Kurt, and he looked back at me.

I got no response, so I kept going: "It is only twenty-five dollars for a two-hour session, and the picture of the host looks normal. Have you used Meetup.com before?"

"No, but I've heard of it. How do you know it is legit?" he asked. It was a good question.

"I don't, but I read the reviews. It seems on the up-and-up. Here, look!" I said as I shoved my laptop on him. Kurt took a look and agreed that there were no immediate red flags. "You can use PayPal. Do you know what that is?" I asked.

"Yeah, I can help you set up an account," he said as he handed me back my laptop.

"But is it trustworthy?" I asked, worried about who I gave my Visa information to. Kurt didn't seem concerned and said, "Yes, it is a pretty well-known system, babe. From my experience, you can trust it." He smiled at me with a look that said, *I can't believe that you have never heard of PayPal before!*

Armed with this new knowledge, I went to create my accounts on Meetup.com and PayPal. Within the hour, I was registered for the development circle that was scheduled just a few weeks later in the month.

It was February of 2014. The first night of class greeted me with cold, dark, and rainy weather. It was not a good mix for someone with night blindness. I was driving on a two-lane road with next to no streetlights. It felt like I was just asking for trouble.

The host's name was Sheila Cash. She provided her home address after payments were made. She also provided parking instructions that I failed to read until after I was already there. Sheila lives in what I like to call a *forest*. To get there, you have to drive on a really scary two-lane road that twists and turns and has little hills that block your view. If someone drives over the dividing line, they are screwed. On one side of the road, there are trees—big, beautiful, glorious trees. On the other side are irrigation ditches. There are also deer lurking in the shrubs. There are streetlights, but they are few and far between.

Nevertheless, I went with my bad night vision and held on to the steering wheel for dear life while being blinded by oncoming vehicles. And I was doing all this while trying to read ridiculously small street signs and listen to my cars navigation system tell me to make a legal U-turn. After a couple of tries, I turned onto the correct street and made it to a set of mailboxes near what appeared to be a road leading to a dead end. *Great, what now?*

After driving up and down that street a few times, I saw two women pull up and get out of a car they had parked right in front of the mailboxes. I rolled down my window, which didn't help me see them any better, and said, "Excuse me, is this where the class is tonight?" They both responded at the same time. "For Sheila? Yes." I thanked them, parked in front of their car, and began walking down the single-lane road.

The road opened up to two homes. Because the two women didn't bother to wait for me, I had no idea which one was Sheila's. I blamed them because it felt better then blaming myself for not reading the parking instructions that included all this information. I couldn't see the house numbers from the road, so I just stood there for a moment, hoping someone else would come by. I was in luck: just as I was cursing myself out, a car pulled up.

It was Steve and his wife, people I formally met when we got inside. They pointed to Sheila's house, and we all walked to the front door together. The outside of her home was beautiful, and I couldn't wait to get inside.

I walked in ahead of Steve and his wife, who brought Sheila flowers. We walked through the front door and into the entryway. The formal dining room was on our right, stairs leading up to the second floor were straight ahead of us, and a living room with a fireplace was to our left.

We were immediately greeted by our host, and she gave Steve and his wife a huge hug. She then turned to me and introduced herself. "Hi. Welcome. I'm Sheila, what is your name?"

"Hi, Sheila, I'm Rena Huisman. This is my first class," I said a little nervously. "Hi, Rena, it's nice to meet you," she said as we shook hands. "Please find a seat; we will get started shortly." She motioned to the living room where there were already half a dozen students sitting.

There were various types of chairs set up in a circle that included a large sofa in the back of the room. It sat underneath a large window that overlooked the large backyard. There was also a coffee table in front of the sofa that featured several lit candles. I found a chair close to the front door. I guess I figured it would be easy to run if I got scared.

As the start time arrived, Sheila began with an orientation for those of us who didn't know her. She provided her background as a medium and the basic format of the class. This included a reminder that her class was not the place for doom and gloom—for example, if someone in the circle picked up information about a cheating spouse, they were asked not share it. I was relieved that there were guidelines. You would be surprised at the number of people who love to share bad news.

As the room filled up, I saw that we were a mixed bag of students: mostly women, but different ages and backgrounds. I was happy to be there, and I felt like I had finally found *my people.*

After orientation, Sheila turned off all the lights, leaving only the candles to light the room. Next, she asked us to get comfortable and close our eyes as she led us through a meditation to help us relax and open up to the highest vibration. It was also done to protect us during our work with spirit.

As we sank into our seats, Sheila began playing a large, crystal singing bowl. The sound vibrated smoothly across the room. At her auditory prompt, we began to hum, keeping our teeth together and lips closed.

After a few minutes, Sheila stopped playing the singing bowl, causing us to stop humming. This is when she opened the floor up for messages. "Please feel free to begin sharing any messages that you receive. They may be for the whole group, or they may be for a specific individual. The message could be from a loved one in spirit or from a higher source such as a guide or an angel. Let's take a few deep, cleansing breaths and begin." Her voice was smooth and mellow. This was kind of funny because, when she wasn't walking us through a meditation, it sounded a bit like a little girl's voice.

I took a few deep breaths and relaxed completely. It didn't take long before I started to receive information, but it felt like the spirits were checking me out, not trying to relay a message, so I remained quiet. Several of the other students began sharing their messages with the group. Some were visions with no particular person attached to them. I was receiving several messages of my own.

Part way through the first hour, one of the women sitting across the room from me started complaining that she was picking up anxiety from someone else in the room that was human not spirit.

"Okay, someone in here must be really nervous, because I am picking up their anxiety. Please stop because it is making my heart race!" *Wow, that was rude.* Her voice was condescending. I had seen and heard a lot over the years, but that was a first. I wanted to tell her to calm down and quit calling people out, but then my heart started racing. *What the? Now they are going to think it's me!*

It came over me like a wave, completely out of nowhere. I tried to relax and let it move through me, but then the woman next to me said, "Now I feel it. Whoever it is needs to calm down!" *Great, now we have two rude women talking smack.*

After she finished complaining I tried to figure out where it was coming from, and what was causing it. I knew *I* wasn't nervous; I was completely relaxed when it hit me, so my first thought was that it must be a spirit that was moving around the room. If it came close enough, its energy could cause one of us to get a sudden bout of anxiety. I just couldn't imagine blaming it on someone else like that.

I concentrated on the vibration until I found the culprit. There was a little girl with us. She was about ten years old and wearing a white nightgown. She had long blonde hair that fell into curly locks down her back. I saw her several more times during that year.

As the second hour ended, Sheila began to close down the circle by saying, "We are now coming to the end. Please take a moment to share any last messages, thoughts, or images that may be lingering in your subconscious with the group."

If you had been seeing giraffes standing behind someone, or a song kept playing in your head, or you kept seeing a pearl necklace with a heart hanging off of it, it was the appropriate time to share these visions with the group to see whether they applied to anyone.

Sheila closed the circle by thanking all the spirits who joined us that evening. She also reminded us to psychically close down and ground ourselves before we left and got behind the wheel. For me, this means that I close each chakra from the base up to the crown, and then I pull my aura in close to me like a warm blanket. I would be lying if I said I didn't leave her house loopy a few times because I forgot to close myself down. I was very lucky that I didn't end up in a ditch.

My first reading was with a spirit of an older man. "I see an older man, maybe in his late sixties. He has tan skin from working outside. It's leathery looking. He has a buzz cut and looks like he is in the military. I see an anchor, so it could be the navy, but he is wearing a leather jacket like a pilot. I see planes; he flew planes in the military." The room was quiet, but I kept seeing his face right in front of me, so I knew I wasn't making it up. And then Sheila asked, "Can he tell you what year it is?" I had no idea, so I asked him. He said, "Forty-two, my year was forty-two." I shared that answer with the group. And that's when one of the women spoke up: "I think that is my father. He flew planes for the navy during that time, but I'm not speaking to him." *What?* Sheila gently encouraged her to hear the message.

Her father wanted her to know that he was with her and said, "We have a lot in common. I don't want you to turn out like me." Those words triggered a response from her of laughter and acknowledgment. I guess it was something that she had never thought of before.

On another occasion, there were three of us sitting in the front of the room in chairs. Dawn was sitting to my left and Sandra was sitting to my right. Sandra said to Dawn, "I see a little girl around you. She is about four years old with blonde hair. She is standing next to your legs." I couldn't see her. Dawn asked, "Can she tell you her name?" Sandra said, "No, I can't get it." I then heard the name *Abby* pop into my head. I said, "I think her name is Abby." Dawn then said, "Oh my God! Abby is a little girl I was very close to who passed away. She was four." We all stared at each other.

I couldn't see her, but I could hear her. Sandra couldn't hear her, but she could see her. Dawn, who is an incredible medium and empath, couldn't see or hear her. And we were all sitting right next to each other. Crazy, huh?

One evening seemed to be animal night. They were everywhere. At least half of the group could see them. There was a reddish-brown horse with a large, white diamond on its forehead that came to visit its owner.

I got the chills when I saw a giant snake the size of a boa constrictor lying across the ground by one woman's feet. When I mentioned it, she wasn't surprised at all. Apparently, it was one of her animal guides. There were also rabbits sitting by Steve, and a flock of different types of birds including what I call a *Baretta bird*. The bird's name comes from a crime show in the seventies called Baretta. The main character had one as a pet. This one was a white cockatoo that was a childhood pet of one of the people in the circle.

One of my biggest challenges besides remote viewing is getting a name. Sheila pushed us to *feel* into the vibration and try to identify each spirit by name. I think this is a challenge for a lot of mediums. For instance, I will *hear* the name *Mike*, so I say, "I hear the name Mike." But then the receiver says, "No, the person that I believe you are talking about is not named Mike." But because of the validated messages that I had already provided, we both knew we had the same person despite the name discrepancy. You have to really *listen* and *feel* into the name at the same time. My percentage rate doing this is still pretty low, and when I do hear it correctly, I never open my mouth for fear of being wrong. See how this messes with your mind?

As I continued to go to the development circle each month, my abilities became sharper. I began to channel more freely and with more confidence. I also became friends with several of the other students, which made the circles even more fun.

A few times, we had new people join us that in my opinion weren't there to learn. They were just there for a reading. You have to admit, twenty-five dollars is a great price for a room full of mediums, psychics, and healers.

One of them was named Brian. He was a nice, intellectual-looking guy with glasses in his forties. He introduced himself and settled right in. It was a full house that evening, and we were running out of space. Sheila had to keep adding chairs.

As the group started sharing messages, I could see a woman appear. She was older with dingy, greasy hair. She was heavy set and wore a shoddy, light-colored muumuu. I got the impression that she was not a very clean person. As I watched her, trying to gather more information to help identify who she was and who she was there to speak to, some of the other members were getting messages for Brian. The majority of them involved his relationship with his wife, a dilemma he was facing.

One of the women in the group, Betty, told Brian that she felt a mother presence around him. He confirmed that his mother was in spirit. And then she relayed a message from her indicating that she was with him and trying to help him. He looked skeptical.

While she was talking, I could hear a train roaring down the tracks at high speed. When Betty came to a stopping point, I asked, "Do you work with trains?" Brian looked over at me and said, "Yes, I do. I have model trains. I collect them." I then knew that the woman who was still standing to my side belonged to him.

"I see a woman. She is wearing a dingy, old muumuu and

slippers. She has greasy, gray hair. Is this your mother?" I asked, a bit worried about the negative description. "Yes, that's her! She always wore those giant dresses."

"Sorry, Brian, but I also got the impression that she wasn't the cleanest or nicest person."

Brian smiled. "You are correct. She didn't shower as often as she should have." I smiled, but I knew there was more to come. "I feel like she said exactly what she felt, even if it hurt the people around her ... including you." He concurred.

I paused to gather more information from the spirit. During this time, Betty shared some additional information with Brian. She suggested that the train had something to do with his journey with his wife or family, but I felt the complete opposite.

About that time, I kept seeing a tree. It was the same tree that was in a large picture above my grandparents' kitchen table. I couldn't remember the name, so I asked the group: "I keep seeing this tree. It is all by itself. It is famous; it was in a picture at my grandparents' house. Does anyone have any ideas?" No one did. So I sat there with this vision sitting right in front of my face and driving me crazy.

As Betty continued sharing her information with Brian, it hit me: "I got it! It's called the Lone Cypress!" Brian looked shocked. "Brian, did you take a vacation with your wife to Pebble Beach?" The answer blew me away. They did vacation there earlier in their marriage when they were happy, and they had a picture standing right in front of the Lone Cypress. *Bingo!*

This is when all the parts and pieces floating around in my head fell into place. "Brian, I don't feel like the train is a message about your journey with your wife. I feel like it is a message to you from your mom telling you to get off the tracks because the train is coming through! Do you understand that?" I asked. "Yes, I do," he answered.

I went on providing the information from his mom that was now flowing easily. It basically came down to the fact that he had to be a man and make a decision. The relationship was unhealthy, and he deserved to be happy.

There was additional information provided by Betty, and then we moved on. After class, Brian came up to me and asked, "Rena, can I give you a hug?" I said, "Sure!" And then gave him a huge hug. "You really helped me tonight," he said. "My mom was not the nicest person, but it was really great to hear from her. I needed her honest advice." We never saw Brian again.

In addition to the once-a-month development circles, Sheila held a psychic development tele-class every Sunday evening. I loved this class! With today's technology, she could set us up in pairs or small groups for our exercises and easily bring us back together for group sharing. It was just as effective as meeting in person.

Each week, there was a different topic such as body scans, messages from friends and loved ones, and messages from guides (including animals). It was a blast. I especially enjoyed it because I didn't know anything about the people I was working with except their first name. There were no preconceived ideas based on what they looked like. In my opinion, it made the readings easier because it was like working with a blank slate. I received the information, and then I shared the information. It was as simple as that. The worst that could happen was the person wouldn't recognize it, but at least I didn't have to see their expression and wonder whether they were lying about it.

It was during this tele-class that I finally felt like my psychic and mediumship abilities were moving to the next level. I was using all the information I had learned over the last ten years and applying it to my readings. I even used numerology and astrology when I felt a pull to a particular astrological sign or number. I used my knowledge of the chakras and auras when conducting body scans. There were even times that I felt that the assistance of a specific crystal or a sea salt bath would be beneficial.

If we wanted, we could use our tarot or oracle cards, but I never did. Instead, I stuck to my little amoeba people that I drew on paper.

They started out as stick people, but then they morphed into things that resembled chubby gingerbread men. Eventually, they became amoeba people.

I wrote the receiver's name down, and then I drew the amoeba person underneath. I waited patiently as the information began to flow through me as I wrote it down. This included circling areas on the head and body that required attention, such as a leg or a hip. I also picked up emotional challenges within the chakra system. Sometimes, I channeled affirmations for them to say to themselves based on that information. It was so much fun!

As if all that wasn't enough, Sheila provided personal development classes (private lessons) once per week, and yes, I took those too. We spent an hour and a half working with different tools of the trade to hone our skills, such as psychometry, giving a reading from a photo, and scrying (looking into a reflective surface such as a crystal ball or mirror to obtain messages through visions).

The first time that I tried to scry, we used a black scrying mirror that was about eight inches in diameter. It gave me just enough reflection to work with. It was actually pretty cool—a little creepy, but cool. I wrote this journal entry when I got home:

> Today in class with Sheila, I was visited by a few guides. The first I met was the doorkeeper to Avalon. Merlin was there. He had a long, white beard and a white robe that was tied around the waist. I was told to return to magic and alchemy, and to work with plants and flowers for it to start coming back to me. They showed me a book that had a red leather cover. The pages had symbols and writing that I could not read. I was told that, once I began working with magic, flowers, plants, and herbs, it would come back to me. I could go back anytime to visit and work with Merlin.

The second guide was a kachina. He was painted white with turquoise stripes and dots of red appeared around his neck and on the feathers or pieces of wood coming out of the top of his rectangular mask. He called me Star Child. He said it was because I could speak to the stars. He also said I could go through doorways between the living and the dead. Before he left, he smiled at me, looked at the moon, and called me Moon Child.

There was a third guide. She appeared to be Egyptian. She was beautiful, but she had an elongated head. She was looking outward, but I couldn't see what she was looking at. She was standing in a type of doorway, and everything around her was made of light brown bricks. I was staring at her, and without turning her head, she asked, "Why are you staring at me?" It shocked me! I immediately looked down at my feet and explained that I meant no disrespect. My sense was that she was very bored. She sighed, glanced my way, and continued to look outward. She said she foresaw the birth and rebirth process. Her name was Hodra or something like that. I got the impression that she didn't like my clothes, the way I was dressed (jeans, vans, t-shirt). She wasn't impressed with woman's future clothing.

None of the information I received was in my stream of consciousness that day, week, or month. The topics were not something I was studying, reading about, or watching on TV, which made it all the more interesting.

About every month and a half, Sheila held a "PsyChicks" meeting. It was a little extra for her students that took personal development classes. And as the name implies, it was for women. The exercises were similar to the ones in our private lessons, but they also included using billets and table tipping. Unfortunately, I never had the opportunity to participate in the table tipping, but I did work with billets. Billets are basically small pieces of paper with the names of deceased love ones or questions for the medium. They are folded several times or rolled up so that the information inside cannot be seen.

There are several ways to perform a billet reading. In our class, Sheila wrote each of our names on a small piece of paper, folded them several times, and placed them in a deep bowl. When it was our turn, Sheila had us pick up one of the folded pieces of paper. We held the folded paper in our hands and began sharing the information that we received with the group. When we were done, we opened it up to reveal the name and validate the information we received.

During a different exercise, Sheila used two bowls. One bowl had our names on the folded pieces of paper. The second bowl had a specific topic, such as relationship, health, business, etc. When it was our turn, we picked a name and a topic. This time, we opened each one to know what we were giving a reading for and to whom, but we weren't given any time to think. We just put the topic and the receiver's name out to the universe and waited for the information to channel through us. It worked really well.

One evening, we were practicing psychometry when we ran into a fun story from one of the PsyChicks named Helen. I randomly selected Helen's name from the bowl right before the reading. We were asked to bring a few objects from home that belonged to a friend or loved one in spirit to use in class, but none of us knew what the others brought, which made it a surprise.

When it was my turn, Helen handed me a very old ring. It was tarnished and missing whatever diamond, pearl, or jewel it held at one time. In addition, one of the prongs was missing, and all the others were bent. I held it in my hand and waited.

I could feel a girl full of spirit who was outspoken and excited. She was in a rush to leave. I saw a gravel road and heard the sound of tires rolling at high speed over the top of it. And then I saw a faint shadow of the back of a vehicle with bright red taillights. It was going down the road at night when I heard the word *wedding*. A moment later, it came together like a small burst of adrenaline in my chest: she was eloping! She was sneaking out of the house to run off with her boyfriend!

As the information came in, I shared it with Helen. But she said, "No, the ring belonged to my grandmother, who, to my knowledge, did not elope." Her response surprised me. "Are you sure? I can't get the scene out of my head," I said as I continued to rattle off more details about the girl's personality. She sat there thinking before saying, "Actually, that sounds like my grandma's sister. She was the rowdy one. And now that I think about it, there were stories about how she snuck out of her window one night and ran off with some guy. I think they found her a few days later."

She went on to link the details of the reading with the stories she remembered, as we all listened. Both of the women were in spirit, so she couldn't ask them. I guess her grandmother's sister really wanted to share her story with us that night ... or maybe there was more to that ring than we would ever know.

As the months went on, I received an e-mail indicating that John Holland was going to be teaching an advanced mediumship course in Portland, Maine, in May. I was interested because it was for advanced students and geared toward working mediums. Plus, I had a feeling it would include platform mediumship. *If it does,* I thought, *I might be ready to give it a try.*

It would require a short flight, a rental car, and a hotel, but I figured it would be a nice getaway. So I ran it by Sheila to make sure I wouldn't miss any of her classes during that weekend. I was lucky: there wasn't a scheduling conflict. She encouraged me to go and have a good time.

When you first meet Sheila, you immediately want to hug her. At least I did. She is both beautiful and kind—and not the kindness that says, *I have to be nice to you because you are in my house.* She exhibits the sincere sort of kindness that flows directly from her heart to yours. Once you get to know Sheila, you realize that she is a lot of fun. She is also the mother of three older children, so she knows her stuff. Throw in a bottle of wine and some good food, and you have the perfect nonjudgmental woman that you love spending time with.

What I Learned in Class

- All my former instructors were right: consistently attending a development circle helps you fine-tune your psychic and mediumship skills.
- Giving a reading over the phone (in tele-classes) with no preconceived ideas is awesome!
- Sheila needs to create meditation CDs because her voice is magical.
- Meetup.com isn't so sketchy after all.
- PayPal is really convenient.

Advanced Mediumship Workshop with John Holland

Over the years, the melasma on my face began to fade. It was still there, but I wasn't hiding indoors as much as I used to. Still, there were times when I thought it looked significantly darker. Allegedly, the severity was linked to my hormones.

"Kurt, do the spots on my face look like they got darker? Look, they seem darker, right?" I ask in desperation. Kurt takes a moment and responds, "What? No, babe, they do *not* look darker. You're beautiful. Quit staring at yourself in the mirror." Kurt is a good liar.

With Sheila's support and Kurt's continued compliments, I went ahead and attended the advanced mediumship workshop with John Holland at the Stage Neck Inn in York, Maine, in May of 2014.

The weekend of John's class was one of those times when the spots on my face appeared darker, especially the ones on my upper lip. I looked like an old man. To add to the problem, I had just switched moisturizer and face makeup before the trip, which was a really bad idea. I was still trying to figure out if they made things better or worse. In short, the trip started off with a new found self-confidence in my psychic and mediumship abilities thanks to Sheila, but I was overly self-conscious about my melasma.

Kurt dropped me off at the airport. "I'm going to miss you, babe. Have fun and call if you need anything. I will keep my phone on me at all times," he promised, and then he gave me a hug and kiss goodbye. I wanted to run back into the truck, but I knew I needed the trip to feel confident about traveling alone again.

The flight went well. We had a delay due to maintenance issues with the plane, but I had my Kindle to entertain me. When we landed, I had a forty-five-minute drive to York from the Portland Airport. The traffic was minimal and the scenery beautiful.

I arrived at the Stage Neck Inn in time for registration at six. The inn sat right on the water in York Harbor. I couldn't think of a better place to hold a class. As I was checking into my room, I asked about a place to eat because I was starving. It turned out that I had just enough time to request a sandwich from the restaurant before they closed. They even offered to have it delivered to my room while I was in class that evening.

After placing my order with the restaurant, I went over to the class registration area inside the conference room. We received a folder full of class materials and a name badge. I brought my own notebook to take notes during class and to journal each night. The main conference room was a good size for the amount of people in the class. It had a beautiful view of the harbor along the back and one side of the room. There were chairs set up in two main sections, all facing the stage with an aisle down the middle. The stage held a small table, chair, easel, and wicker basket.

The wicker basket was used to hold questions from the students throughout the weekend. An index card was placed in our packets so we could submit a question for John to answer during the class. The question had to be related to giving readings or working as a medium.

That evening, John began class with introductions, an overview of the class schedule, and a layout of the Stage Neck Inn. After a brief question–and–answer session—but before we began our first exercise—John asked everyone to raise their hands if they were professional mediums. They didn't have to do it as a full-time job, but if they were giving readings consistently and getting paid for them, they were considered professionals. Hands flew up.

And then he reversed it and asked everyone to raise their hands if they were not professional mediums. The numbers shocked me. Out of at least fifty people in the class, there were only two of us who were not professionals. I wasn't sure whether that was good or bad.

Shortly thereafter, we went into our first exercise of the evening. "Everyone grab a partner. We are going to begin our readings. Make sure you have plenty of space between you and the people next to you," John advised. The whole class got up and began moving chairs into different areas of the room for privacy.

I grabbed the guy sitting next to me, Troy. We moved our chairs so that we were facing each other, and then we waited for John's instructions. I have to admit, it was a little uncomfortable facing a complete stranger and trying not to stare or have a conversation.

"Decide who will be the medium and who will be the receiver," John said as he walked around the room to make sure we were all ready. "When I say begin, the medium will start the reading. The receiver will only answer *yes* or *no*. Try not to share any other information until I call time." The chatter in the room escalated with all the excitement.

We agreed that Troy would be the medium first, so all I had to do was sit there, be open, and relax. "Okay, is everyone ready?" John asked. "Begin!"

After those words, the room exploded. I could hear voices all around me talking at the same time.

"Rena," Troy began, "I feel a gentleman with you, a grandfather. Do you have a grandfather in spirit?" he asked.

"Yes," I replied.

"I feel like he is with you, guiding you. I feel like you were close and are very similar."

I said, "Yes," which was partly true. He is a guide of mine, but we were not close when he was alive. I admit that we are similar in that we are both moody control freaks, so I also gave him that. Plus, he looked nervous, and I wanted to help him out.

The medium was also supposed to try to pick up information

about the receiver, so Troy switched his focus. "I believe you may work with technology," he said.

I answered, "Yes," but it kind of ended there.

"Okay, let's begin to wrap it up," John announced as he continued to walk around the room. "Take a moment to validate the information with the receiver before switching places."

Troy asked me about the information he received, and I provided him with the details. We laughed about it as we settled in for my turn.

"All right, let's switch places now. Is everyone ready?" John asked. We all nodded our heads. "Begin!"

Immediately, I started drawing my little amoeba person. I put Troy's name on top in my journal as the information began coming in. "Troy, I'm going to read you first, and then let's see who comes through to visit, okay?" Troy nodded as he watched me draw and scribble notes in my journal.

> **Me**: "Okay, from a quick scan, I feel that you are having problems with your eyes, specifically your right eye."
> **Troy**: "Yes."
> **Me**: "I also feel that you are experiencing issues with your left leg and hip area."
> **Troy**: "Yes."
> **Me**: "I feel like it is related to an accident, a fall."
> **Troy**: "Yes."
> **Me**: "When it comes to your job, I see dollars and cents, so I feel like it is financial. I also see spreadsheets, like you handle some kind of financial metrics for your company. At the same time, I feel like you are surrounded by technology. Do you work for Oracle or a company like that?"
> **Troy**: *He just sat there staring at me. So I went on.*
> **Me**: "I also feel like you have the luck of the Irish with you. Are you Irish? Or do you know what this means?"
> **Troy**: "Yes."

Me: [I thought, *Good, at least I know he is paying attention.*]
"One last thing, I can feel your heart chakra. There is
an affirmation that I am receiving for you: I look and
feel amazing. I am love. I give love. I get love. Do you
understand this?"

Troy: "Yes."

Before John called time, Troy's grandmother and grandfather
came through to assure him that he was not alone and that they
supported *his* decision.

After John called time, Troy confirmed that he worked with
spreadsheets and created financial metrics for his company. He
noted that he was getting headaches from vision problems related
to his right eye. He also stated that he was getting over issues
from an accident that impacted his left leg and caused discomfort
in his left hip. The heart chakra message was related to recent
relationship issues. The message from his grandparents was related
to the relationship situation as well. He was Irish.

Unfortunately, I had to pull this information out of him. It was like
he didn't want to admit it was right. Maybe my little amoeba person
freaked him out. It shouldn't have—after all, we were sitting in an
advanced mediumship class—but he appeared surprised by it all. I was
surprised by my reading too, but his reservations really pissed me off.

After a short question-and-answer session, we exchanged a few
more readings with other partners before the evening activities ended.

When I went back to my room, I found an amazing bacon,
ham, and cheese sandwich with chips and a Diet Coke waiting for
me. I was famished, which made the food even more awesome. I
wolfed it down while processing the events that evening.

I felt good about the exercises. I was very relaxed giving each
reading. I wanted a beer to celebrate that thought, but I decided
against it. Instead, I read my book and fell asleep.

The next morning, everyone met downstairs in the restaurant
for a tasty buffet breakfast. I settled on scrambled eggs, bacon,

potatoes, and toast. It was magical. I did my best to stay away from anything sugary to avoid a stomachache or headache during our exercises. We had a long day ahead of us, and I didn't want to spend it feeling ill.

John began the day with an overview of the night before. We moved on to review some of the class materials in our folders as he mixed in his own personal experiences and challenges giving readings. I was sitting in the very back row, where it was nice and comfortable with a cool breeze from the air conditioner. Also, I didn't have to worry about interrupting anyone if I had to get up.

There was an older woman sitting to my right, wearing multiple layers of clothing. She had a tote bag and a gigantic purse with her that could have doubled as a suitcase. Every now and then, she started digging through it and making a bunch of noise as if she were stomping through a pile of dry leaves.

The first time she did it was for some sort of lip balm. The second was for medication. And then I lost track. It became extremely distracting, and I was really starting to get irritated. One of the women sitting directly in front of her turned around to figure out what the problem was, but the woman sitting next to me didn't get the hint.

While I struggled to hear John and keep my patience in check, she did the unexpected: she dug in, pulled out a nail file, and began filing her fingernails. I couldn't believe it. It was so weird that I wanted to laugh … but I was too annoyed. I also wanted to stab her with her fingernail file, but I just turned around and glared at her until she finally looked up instead.

"Oh, I'm sorry, but I have this nail that keeps snagging on my sweater." She said, while looking at me like I should understand. I didn't.

"I see that, but I can't hear what John is saying," I replied, trying very hard not to sound confrontational. But then it got worse.

Less than ten minutes later, she put the file away and started searching for something new. It was so obnoxious that I put my forehead in my hands while trying to find the right words. She must have seen me and the look on the woman's face to her other side, because she pushed her chair back about two feet. *What now?*

Apparently, when you push your chair back a few feet, no one can hear you digging through your purse anymore. *This woman is insane …*

When I thought it couldn't get any worse, she did the mother of all rude deeds: she started clipping her fingernails. *Snap! Snap! Snap! Snap! Are you fucking kidding me?* My head exploded. "Lady, are you serious?" She just sat there staring at me. I wanted to pick up her purse and throw it across the room, but I couldn't. I was so pissed off that I pushed *my* chair back, got up, and walked straight out the door to the restroom. I paced back and forth and said the f-word about three hundred more times until I calmed down.

Unfortunately, she was not the first moron I had run into in a class, but she was definitely the most distracting next to the fingernail typist in the writer's workshop.

Eventually, I went back into the classroom, but I did not return to my seat. I stayed in the back of the room standing by the refreshment table looking outside at the water. It was almost time for break. I was so mad that it was hard to contain my facial expressions. I noticed that a few of the other women around her had gotten up as well.

During break, I went outside for some fresh air. That is when I met a woman named Carla. Apparently, I wasn't the only one who was annoyed by a person sitting nearby. We shared our stories and had a good laugh before it was time to go back in. Who knew commiserating could be so healing? When I went back inside, I sat down in a different chair far away from the bag lady. I managed to avoid her for the rest of the weekend without even trying.

Before lunch, we broke into groups of three to give readings. Two people were the readers for the third person, taking turns as they received information. Therefore, it gave each person two opportunities to give a reading. I paired up with two other women.

Things were moving along, and we were all working well together. And then we came to the last person in the group. I was one of the readers. My partner and I were picking up messages from adults, but then I felt the spirit of a little boy come in.

"I can feel a little boy around you, maybe five years old," I said. "Yes," she said. The feeling was getting stronger.

"Is it your grandson or nephew?" I asked. It didn't feel like it was her son.

"Yes," she said. And then I saw a potato, just like the ones in the grocery store, but bigger.

"He is showing me a potato. Do you know what this is?" I asked. She shrugged her shoulders. But then I saw the potato again. It was underground this time, surrounded by dirt. I had no idea what it meant. It was very strange.

"He is showing me the same potato, but it is still underground and surrounded by dirt," I said. And then I saw her facial expression change. "Does this mean anything to you?"

"Yes," she said, "give me a moment."

It turned out that her nephew was buried alive. It was his way of showing me the way he died—like a potato buried underground. In that moment, being a medium felt horrible.

After that group exercise, we took a welcomed two-hour break for lunch. It was provided by the establishment on the covered patio. We sat around large, round tables getting to know each other a little better without sharing too much information. We knew we couldn't be too detailed, because we might have to give each other a reading later. This seems to be the unspoken rule in these sorts of classes, especially information about deceased family, friends, or pets. Instead, we stuck with high-level topics such as classes we had attended, supernatural experiences we had in or out of class, other instructors, and that kind of stuff. It was really entertaining despite being impersonal. This worked well for me because my life was pretty boring.

The second part of class was focused on platform mediumship.

John gave us an opportunity to volunteer by raising our hands, but he also picked students randomly to get up on stage and give a reading as well. I knew I wanted to do it, but I was still nervous about volunteering right away. I wanted to get a feel for how things worked before I went up there. Lucky for me, I didn't hear my name until the last half of class.

John was in the process of providing feedback to the woman who just finished giving a reading. I was sitting right in the middle of the room, out in the open with no one to hide behind, when he looked right at me. *Oh no.* "Rena, come on up," John said.

I stumbled onto the stage while John handed me the mic, which felt surprisingly heavy. I guess that sensation was a side effect of feeling nervous and near fainting.

The mic trembled in my hand like a twenty-pound weight. "It's going to be okay, you can do this. Take a few breaths and relax. When you feel ready, go ahead and begin." John said, as I looked out into the fifty-plus sets of eyes staring back at me. *Oh my God, don't faint. Rena, please don't faint.*

Right about the time I was going to drop the mic and run, I felt a woman coming close to me. She felt soothing like a grandmother, and I began to talk. "I feel a woman with me, a grandmother energy, a strong woman." Half of the room held up their hands. I nodded in acknowledgment so they could put them down.

I noticed that I couldn't stop looking toward the back of the room at a specific group of people, so I went with that. "I feel like she is connected to someone sitting in the back of the room to my right, in that area," I said and pointed in that direction. "She is showing me a hospital and an ambulance." A dozen hands went up again. I nodded and they put them down.

"She went to the hospital in an ambulance. I feel pain in my chest, heart failure or some other heart related problem that she was aware of," I explained. Another dozen hands went up. Again, I nodded.

At this point, people were trying to make the reading fit their relatives when it didn't. I could tell by the way it *felt*, that this spirit was not related to them. The information I was getting was very high level, so I asked the spirit for more details when I got a clear sign.

"Okay," I said. "She also *worked* at a hospital; she was a nurse." I felt like I was finally getting somewhere. And that was when a woman sitting in the very back of the room on my right raised her hand. Someone then handed her a mic so the class could hear both sides of the conversation.

"She is my grandmother. She was a nurse at a hospital. She died of a heart attack, but she had a known heart condition. She was taken to the hospital by ambulance," she explained. I wanted to drop to my knees and say *hallelujah*!

This is about the time that John stepped in because, apparently, I was pausing a lot while I was gathering the information in my head. He encouraged me to go off stage and walk over to the recipient. I did that, but it threw me off for a moment.

"Hi, I'm Rena. What is your name?" I asked. "Kelly," she said as I started receiving more information.

"I also feel a mother energy. Is your mother in spirit as well?" I asked.

"Yes," she replied.

"Are you a nurse too? I feel like you didn't know your grandmother well, but you are told you are a lot like her."

"Yes, I am. And yes, I hear that a lot."

This is when John stepped in again, pushing me to get a message from spirit for Kelly. I guess I wasn't moving fast enough, because he also began helping the reading along by providing the message that he was receiving. *Um … I thought I was the student.*

John's message for her was along the same line as the one I was receiving, but I also received information about her brother that I didn't get an opportunity to share. My classmates applauded as I handed the mic back to John. I thanked Kelly before walking back to my seat. There was some quick feedback from John about pacing the reading, and then he moved on to the next victim.

I did it! I really did it! And I didn't faint, throw up, or wet myself. I felt really good despite the fact that I still couldn't feel my legs. I was awesome!

Several of the other students gave readings on stage before we took a break for dinner. But that day's events were not over. Later that evening, we had student gallery readings from eight to ten o'clock. John invited the family and friends of the students to attend the event. This meant that whomever volunteered or was selected would have additional nonstudent audience members to work with. It was not mandatory, but I thought it would be crazy not to show up unless you were one of the students who had not been on stage yet.

A big group of us gathered in the restaurant for dinner at a big, round table. We ate steak, lobster, and oysters with all the sides. The food was expensive but fantastic. We laughed with each other about our readings and looked forward to the student gallery readings because most of us were off the hook.

Unless the students let John know that they would not be participating, they had to be ready to give a reading. You would think that possibility would stop them from drinking at dinner, but it didn't. And when I say drinking, I don't mean a single beer or glass of wine; I mean putting a few bottles of wine away.

I'm not judging, because I love my Miller Lite, but I wouldn't get drunk before giving a reading in front of a large group of strangers. I would wait until afterward and use my success as an excuse to celebrate (which I did later that evening). There is something about slurring while talking to spirit that seems a little disrespectful and stupid. You are just asking to make an ass out of yourself and end up on YouTube.

Anyway, we finished dinner and went back to our rooms to freshen up before the readings began. I changed into some comfy yoga pants, grabbed a fresh bottle of water, and went over to find a seat. The room was filling up fast when I grabbed a chair in the back row. John began with an introduction and welcomed the family and friends who were in the audience. He also gave a short overview of mediumship and what to expect that evening. And then he moved right into selecting the first reader.

The readings started off well, and I was really impressed. Some of the students were obviously nervous, but they let their sense of humor shine through, giving their readings a jump-start and lightening the energy in the room. But then we hit a snag.

John selected one of the women who had a little too much to drink at dinner. I was holding my breath and praying she wouldn't fall as she walked up on stage. John introduced her and handed her the mic. She looked like she was having a hard time focusing. She just stood there staring at her feet, holding the mic between both hands as if she were praying. I know I would have been. And then she started swaying and mumbling fragments of a message, but she couldn't hold on to them long enough to convey anything that made sense. John stepped in to help her along and bring the reading to an end. It was painful to watch. She was a beautiful woman who had a reputation for being a very good medium. It is too bad that was the only demonstration we got to see.

The evening closed on a high note though, with a few of the most talented mediums I had ever seen. Afterward, a small group of us met in the bar for drinks. It was time to celebrate. I limited myself to two beers—after all, we still had one more half day of class, and I didn't want to start it off with a pounding headache.

The next morning, we met downstairs for the breakfast buffet. Everyone seemed to be in a very good mood. We were all ready to go home, and class was scheduled to end at noon. That was after our check-out time, so we brought our bags down for the hotel to hold for us and hung out in the lobby. It was a beautiful, sunny day, so no one was in a hurry to get to class. I wanted to sit in the sunshine by the water and read a book.

John kicked off the last day with a review of everything we worked on. He talked about the student gallery readings the night before and answered several questions that were put into the wicker basket throughout the weekend. My question was never answered. I asked, "How long should we schedule a reading when we are starting out. Thirty minutes? An hour?"

We had one more group exercise before the closing ceremony, and it was one that I was familiar with from my class with James Van Praagh. But this time it had an added twist. We created two long rows with chairs facing each other. When we were done, John asked everyone to sit down. And then he said, "The two rows facing the window, get up and trade places with each other." We all laughed, got up, and found new seats within the other row. "This way, you can't pick who you want to read," he explained. We all giggled because we knew he was right.

"Many of you may have done this before, but we are going to make it a little harder for you," he said as he held up blue, plastic blindfolds. "Here are the rules: the readers will be blindfolded. When they are ready, they will begin asking questions based on the information that they receive. The receivers are not allowed to talk. They can only answer using one tap on the knee for *yes* and two taps for *no*. Based on those cues, the reader will continue."

Once we were wrapped in plastic, John reminded the receivers not to talk and asked them to get up and change seats. Now we really had no idea who we were reading! It sounds insane, but it was kind of a relief. Similar to Sheila's tele-classes, there were no preconceived ideas to get in the way.

Once the receivers were settled, John said the magic word: "Begin." The room came alive. My crazy reading went something like this:

> **Me**: "I see a man dressed in a suit. He's a tall, good-looking man, and the suit defines him. Is this your brother in spirit?"
> **Receiver**: [Two taps for *no*].
> **Me**: "I see another man who feels close to the first one in the suit, but he is a rugged, outdoorsy type and about the same age. They are friends, maybe bothers. Make sense?"

Receiver: [Two taps for *no*].

Me: "The man in the suit collects vintage cars. I know you said *no*, but he keeps coming back.

Receiver: [Tap, tap, tap, tap, tap].

Me: [*What the hell does that mean?*] "Do you know the man in the suit?"

Receiver: [One tap for *yes*].

Me: "Are they both in spirit?"

Receiver: [Two taps for *no*].

Me: "Is the rugged guy in spirit?"

Receiver: [One tap for *yes*].

Me: "Were they brothers? They feel like they spent a lot of time together working on cars and stuff."

Receiver: [Two taps for *no*].

Me: "Were they friends?"

Receiver: [One tap for *yes*].

Me: "This is insane! Ha-ha!"

Right when I was laughing my ass off and ready to throw in the towel, John called time. "Go ahead and remove your blindfolds."

The receiver was a gal with whom I had only a brief conversation all weekend. She was one of those people I felt like I had known my whole life. We were both laughing at how difficult it was.

"I kept tapping on your knee to try to tell you to go back to the original question," she said. "I needed a way to say, 'Yes, I do know who you were talking about.'"

She explained that the man in the suit was her brother, who is still alive. He is a minister who wears suits every day. The other guy was his best friend from childhood, and he passed away recently. They used to work on cars when they were in high school, and her brother has a vintage car. The exercise was a blast, but the blindfold kind of crushed my eyelashes.

We then repeated the exercise, switching roles. Unsurprisingly, I was just as frustrated being the receiver. With only *yes* or *no* answers, I couldn't ask the reader to clarify anything such as a job description or the person's age. This made it difficult for me because I have several dark-haired, tall, brown-eyed uncles who passed away. As the receiver, I couldn't tell which one she was talking about without more details. I went ahead and tapped once for *yes* because it could have been any of them, but we didn't get much further before we ran out of time.

After the exercise, we had our last break before the closing ceremony. When we came back into the room, the chairs were rearranged in a large circle. There was a beautiful candle in a glass vase on a stand sitting in the middle.

I didn't participate in the ceremony, because I had a flight to catch. It was either sit in the airport for four hours or skip the ceremony, it was an easy choice. I went in, said my good-byes, and left.

As I was driving back to the airport, I reviewed the weekend's events. I was really surprised that so many of the students who were full-time mediums were nervous about giving readings on stage or in the group circles. I figured that as a professional reader, they would naturally be more confident. But since I had only given two readings outside of class (not counting the ones that occurred spontaneously at the bar or at the salon), I really didn't know.

I had a great time minus the bag lady. I met really interesting people, heard some brilliant mediums do their thing on stage, and got past my own fear of public speaking for a moment in time. Life was good.

What I Learned in Class

- Getting drunk before giving a reading is not a good idea.
- Do not sit next to women with large tote bags or purses.
- Platform mediumship is terrifying. You have to be batshit crazy to do it—count me in for the next time!
- Blindfolds crush your eyelashes.

Reiki First and Second Degree with Yvonne P. Gleason

After I returned from John Holland's workshop, I stepped back into the groove with my classes with Sheila. A few months later, I started feeling an extra amount of energy in my hands that I wasn't quite sure what to do with. After some thought, I decided it was time to take a class specific to healing.

In September of 2014, I attended a class called Reiki first and second degree with Yvonne P. Gleason at the Reiki Sanctuary of Northern Virginia in Fairfax, Virginia.

I apologize now for leaving out the low-level details specific to Reiki. Please understand that this is done out of respect for the process through which Reiki knowledge is passed from instructor to student.

Before I attended class, the only prior knowledge of Reiki I had was what I gathered from a few books I ordered from Amazon. It seemed very similar to the energy healing that I had learned in other classes, but it included the use of symbols.

Reiki first degree was held on Saturday, and Reiki second degree was held on Sunday. Students could take them both in one weekend or split them up over two weeks like I did. Both classes were held in Yvonne's home. It was small but cozy, and there was plenty of room for two Reiki tables and the five of us (including Yvonne).

We began Reiki first degree with introductions and an overview. Yvonne provided each of us with a personalized binder filled with class materials, a pen, and a book called *Reiki The Healing Touch — First and Second Degree Manual* by William Lee Rand.

Because I always get nervous when asked to introduce myself, I did my best to relax and pay attention. When it was my turn, I said, "Hi, my name is Rena Huisman. I'm here to learn how to work with the energy in my hands." I was asked to clarify, so I said, "I have studied metaphysics for almost ten years, so I am familiar with the chakra system and auras, but I felt that taking a course specific to hands-on healing would be beneficial." Yvonne then asked me about the other classes I attended that included information about the chakra system and auras. I didn't want to answer, but I did: "I have taken classes in mediumship, psychic development, and energy healing." There was a short pause that felt like twenty minutes.

"Wow, so you are psychic?" one of the students asked. "Yes," I replied reluctantly. "Are you a medium? Can you see spirits?" she continued. "Yes, but not professionally," I answered.

This was my canned response that generally worked well for people who believed in mediumship and might want to ask for a reading during class. The *not professionally* part usually throws them off. For the people who don't believe in mediumship, psychic abilities, or are on the fence, it sets their minds at ease if they are afraid that I might be able to read their thoughts. I don't know why people always think that, but they do. I can't read your mind, I promise!

After our introductions were complete, Yvonne shared the definition of Reiki with us, its history, the Usui Reiki lineage, its ideals, the associated affirmations, the main parts of the human energy system and the energy centers of the body. All of this information was provided in our class binder so we could reference it later if necessary.

We moved on to learning the Reiki first degree symbol, which I cannot share. We practiced drawing it, saying the name out loud for proper enunciation, and writing down the meaning. We then took a test that we all passed.

After a short break, Yvonne explained how and when the

symbol was used, and then she walked us through the various hand positions for treating others and self-treatment. They were also depicted in the manual.

Yvonne demonstrated the hand positions for self-treatment on herself as we followed along, and then she demonstrated the hand positions for treating others on one of the students. She moved slowly so we could see the nuances of each one. After the demonstration, we learned how to scan the body for areas that required extra attention (healing)—a process called Byosen scanning. This was similar to what I had learned in other classes when identifying etheric cords.

We held our hands a few inches above the receiver and scanned from head to toe. If we identified hot spots, we sent extra healing energy to those locations. We did this by allowing the healing to come through us from the universe. It traveled down into our crown chakras and out through our hands to the receiver. We can direct the energy, but it will go wherever the body needs it.

It was then time to practice on each other. My partner was Martha. She was a soft-spoken woman who had always been interested in energy healing but never got the chance to attend a class until now. We agreed that she would be the receiver first.

As Martha relaxed on the Reiki table, I followed Yvonne's instructions and scanned the head and neck area first. My hands began to heat up, slightly pulsating in my palms. I didn't identify any hot spots, but I began to pick up information about Martha psychically. I started feeling anguish and stress about an employment situation and sadness surrounding children.

As I moved down her body, I felt pain in one of her hips. I sent extra healing energy into that location as I picked up an overall pain within that leg. I also received the impression that the pain could be lessened with an adjustment to her back. Because it wasn't a psychic development class, and part of the exercise did not include giving the receiver a reading, I cleared my mind and kept going.

When I arrived at Martha's knees, I could see her kneeling

down on the ground in a carpeted room and picking up toys. She felt happy and sad at the same time. I wondered whether the people I sensed were her children, but it felt like there were a lot of them, not just two or three. I sent healing energy to both of her knees while trying to clear my mind.

I heard Yvonne's gentle voice ask us to bring the scan to an end. Afterward, we spent some time sharing our experiences as healers and receivers.

"I could feel heat coming from Rena's hands. My body felt very light and relaxed," Martha said. I thanked her for the feedback. Yvonne then asked me what I experienced. "I felt tension in Martha's neck and pain in her right hip that radiated down. I also felt pain in both knees." I'm not sure that was the answer I was supposed to give judging from the look on their faces. Maybe it was too intrusive, but Martha verified my statement without any obvious look of concern. I kept my mouth shut about the other stuff.

When it was time to switch places, I jumped onto the Reiki table and got comfortable. "This table is magical," I said to Yvonne. "I could lie here all day."

Martha began the scan while I relaxed. I could feel the heat coming from her hands as she moved them across my energy field. She stopped at my left hip and sent it extra healing energy. It was a spot-on assessment—that hip had been giving me problems for years.

Overall, the healing felt very uniform and soothing. It seemed like only a few minutes had gone by when I heard Yvonne's voice asking the healers to begin bringing the exercise to an end. Once again, we shared our experiences as healers and receivers, and then we took a lunch break.

We gathered around Yvonne's kitchen table to eat our sack lunches. I brought a ham sandwich, a stick of string cheese, a granola bar, and some caffeine-free Diet Coke. Martha was sitting across the table from me. Call me nosy, but I asked her about the information I picked up.

"Martha, do you have kids?" I asked, trying to sound nonchalant.

"No. I'm married, but we don't have any children yet. Why?" At that point, I decided to throw caution to the wind.

"Well, when I was conducting the scan and I got to your knees, I could see you picking toys up off the ground in a room with carpet. I could also feel children all around you." Martha chuckled a little while she finished chewing her food.

"Those are my students," she said. "I miss them so much. I think about them every day. It makes me so sad." She explained that she taught preschool, but something went wrong when renewing her work visa, which meant she had to stop teaching until it was straightened out. She loved her job but couldn't do it. I felt her sadness from across the table.

After lunch, we received our first degree healing attunement. I cannot elaborate on what was involved, but I will tell you that I had an interesting experience. This is what I wrote in my journal immediately after it was done:

> I felt like I was floating. I saw all the colors of the chakras spiral together into a type of braided rope vortex that connected with the heavens through my crown chakra. I felt aspects of myself through time. I saw myself being pointed at, laughed at, pulled by the neck with a rope, and ridiculed for what I was, who I was with. Lifetime in the days of castles and motes.
>
> At one point, I felt myself floating up. My hands were lifting up on their own, and my crown chakra was staring to pulsate. I have a dull headache/earache on my left side.
>
> In the last part of the attunement, I saw a dark blue light moving up and down in a straight line. It was like standing in a very large, dark room and seeing a ray of light come straight down the middle with a blue light inside of it. I kept waiting for it to expand left to right, but it didn't.

I was a woman dressed in a blue and white dress. I believe
I had light hair and eyes. It was muddy and cold.

I had a headache for the remainder of the day, but the intensity
died down by the end of the evening.

We were now ready to give each other a full Reiki treatment
using all the hand placements. The process was long, and after
switching partners, it took up the remainder of the day. Between
sessions, we took a short break to share our experiences.

As the healer, I found it very difficult to hold my hands in the
positions for the required amount of time. I am five feet and ten
inches tall, and the table was not tall enough for me. Consequently,
my back began to ache. This distracted me from the treatment. I
tried using the adjustable stool, but I found it awkward to sit down
and just as distracting.

As the receiver, it was a wonderful experience. I fell into a very
deep sleep. I woke myself up a few times when my body twitched.
After the treatment was over, Martha told me that I twitched when
she was sending healing into my hip.

"You scared me when your leg jerked! I jumped back and
focused on not laughing," she said. *That's pretty funny!*

The Reiki second degree class was a lot like the first one, but
we were introduced to crystals and learned additional symbols and
techniques. We also received the second degree healing attunement.
This is what I wrote in my journal immediately after it was done:

> During the Reiki II attunement, I felt the existence of
> the high priestess. When Yvonne touched the top of my
> head, I felt my cap, tall and white above my head. I had
> become the high priestess in a white and light blue gown.
> Quickly after, I was an Indian princess with a headdress,
> and I was in the woods. I turned into a Mayan princess
> at one point as well, remaining in the woods among the
> trees and waterfalls. At one point, I dove into the water

and swam below the surface for a period of time, taking in all that I saw. I felt like they were all with me, but I was one of them at the same time. I felt like a healer, a lover of earth, a seeker, a divine being here to provide assistance where I am called. All their aspects of self are also my own; they are with me, and I am part of them. We all have our missions at different periods in time, and this is mine.

When I left both classes, I felt exhausted and had a pounding headache. This is common when you work with your crown and sixth chakra to channel energy or spirit. This is why I did not take the classes back to back. I was so completely fried after the first class that I asked Yvonne if I could wait a few weeks to take the second one.

I expected to have a transformational experience that I never had. This may be because of all the classes I attended, where I heard a lot of the same information. The main differences were those things specific to Reiki such as the use of symbols, specific hand placements, attunements, and the step-by-step process for a treatment from beginning to end.

To my surprise, I never got an answer for what to do with all the extra energy in my hands. But now, when I feel it, I either stop and meditate on it, send it out to everyone and everything, or make Stitch lay down and channel it into her. She makes a great receiver. I know I am doing a good job when she starts snoring.

What I Learned in Class

- I enjoy using my hands for psychic readings and healings.
- I don't enjoy memorizing a lot of information in order to give a reading or a healing.
- Reiki really works!

Channeling
with Sheila Cash

Sheila had been tossing around the idea of creating a separate class specific to channeling clarity, courage, and authenticity. This type of channeling takes you deeper inside your own psyche. In my opinion, it is very different from mediumship.

There were a handful of us who were interested, but we had to remember that what we channeled could be very personal. This meant that we had to trust that what was said in the circle stayed in the circle.

Sheila set up the first couple of classes in her home. Later, they were moved to the Arlington Metaphysical Chapel (AMC) in Arlington, Virginia, on Tuesday evenings.

During the first class, we channeled authenticity. Because I had never done anything like it before, I was worried. Still, I had already promised myself that I would fully commit to it, and that meant letting go completely.

Sheila started class the same way she did in our development circles. We began with a deep mediation, followed with humming assisted by the crystal singing bowl. Next, she guided us through channeling authenticity in the first person.

Initially, I couldn't speak. It was as if I wasn't in control of my own voice. I also began to *feel* different as I took on authenticity's personality. It was like I was becoming authenticity itself. I know that sounds strange, but that is the only way I can describe it. Here is my journal entry after that experience:

> During channeling class, our focus was authenticity. In the beginning, we channeled authenticity itself and its messages to us in class. We spoke in the first person as authenticity. It was very enlightening. For the second part, we spoke from our authentic self to ourselves in the third person: "As Rena's authentic self, Rena *is* or *wants* or *feels*." I found that my authentic self was a little girl who didn't like boundaries or standing still. She wanted to play and dance! She also craved desire and passion. Out of nowhere, my authentic self said that Rena wanted to dance naked under the full moon! I realized that I need to feel free, that dance is really important to me. So is art and magic. I am magic. It is who I am, and until I cut free and live my authentic self, I will continue to feel frustrated. After class, I was really amped up! It was like I had enough energy for ten people! Thank you, divinity and authenticity! I love and appreciate you all!

I didn't start attending the channeling classes at AMC until October. That was also the last month that Sheila taught any of her development classes in 2014. Because the holiday season was right around the corner, she took the last few months off to spend time with her family and friends. We were lost ... and then it got worse.

After the first of the year in 2015, Sheila decided that it was time to write her book. It was a longtime project that had been sitting on the back burner for a while. Unfortunately for all of us, she decided 2015 was the year to do it. So with a heavy heart but exciting future, Sheila let us know the bad news: she was taking an indefinite break.

It is June 2nd, 2015, as I am writing this chapter. It has been eight months with no development classes, tele-classes, PsyChicks, or channeling sessions in the basement of AMC. I wanted to call Sheila to tell her to hurry up and write her stupid book because we were tired of waiting, but I chickened out and sent her the following text message instead:

> "Hey, Sheila, it's Rena, just wanted to let you know that I miss you. Hope the book is coming along well. HUGS!"

It was more appropriate, plus I didn't want to be on her bad side when she started her classes again. I was thinking ahead.

What I Learned in Class

- Channeling authenticity, courage, clarity, and love takes guts, especially in front of strangers.
- Learning to completely let go and *allowing our feelings* to speak is hard but extremely rewarding. I highly recommend it.
- Sheila is worth the wait.

And That Was the End

Sheila's channeling class marked the end of my ten-year journey. I have to say that it was a perfect ending to a rocky beginning back in 2004. I can't express enough how lucky I feel that I was led down this path and given the means to attend all these classes. Each and every instructor provided pieces to the metaphysical puzzle that was slowly being put together in my mind. I had no idea where it was leading me then, and I still don't know. But it doesn't matter, because there is no way that I am stopping now. In fact, I feel the complete opposite.

I am looking forward to continuing my growth and expanding into deeper realms of consciousness. I believe that we can levitate, bend metals from a distance, move objects with our minds, and heal ourselves and others in moments rather than days. I would love to be able add those abilities to my bag of knowledge in *this* lifetime.

Maybe I will add *teacher* to the long list of things I've done by sharing all the information that was taught to me over the years—those incredibly priceless nuggets of information that I hold so close to my heart. Maybe I will finally step forward, embrace my abilities, and give readings. Or maybe I will continue to hide behind my laptop and write. Only time will tell.

The one thing I know for sure is that, like many of you, I will continue moving forward as a life-long student of the intuitive arts. For *now*, that is perfect.

Afterword

Initially, I began writing this book because I was sick and tired of reading about someone else's happy ending. I had taken the classes, joined the development circles, meditated, and kept up my dream journal. What was I doing wrong? Why wasn't I being called upon to do this work full-time? What am I supposed to do with all this knowledge?

In many of the classes we were given the impression that it was easy. "Just practice on your friends and family," they would say, "before you know it, you will have more business then you know what to do with." But that isn't necessarily the truth.

For one, we don't all have *friends and family* to practice on. I didn't even come out of the Psychic closet until recently. And two, not everyone is qualified to be a professional after just a few classes, certificate or not.

There were many students who flocked to these workshops with the explicit purpose of quitting their day jobs. They thought they were going to come out of class a ready-made, full-blown professional medium. But it wasn't that easy.

There were also students who wanted to be a professional for all the wrong reasons. The focus shouldn't be about making money; it should be about being of service to others. There is no doubt in my mind that some of the most gifted mediums out there are not famous. They don't have a presence online or use social media platforms to promote themselves. They might not even have business cards. Instead, they are tucked away in faraway places, providing their services for a nominal fee or for free. Although he did become famous, we could all take a page out of Edgar Cayce's book by bringing the focus back to *healing*.

I believe that some of us, no matter how intuitive we are, were not meant to use our gifts in a private practice. Sure, we all want to use what we learned, but for the majority of us, we are here to inspire, to raise the vibration of the earth, and to be *undercover lightworkers*.

But with all that said, I still encourage everyone to take more classes. Do it for the sheer fun of being around other intuitive people and for self-growth. It's akin to writers and writer's workshops: it's great to be around like-minded people, your people. That can be more than enough.

In the end, what I found was that writing this book was a calling. It presented me with proof of how much I had learned and grown over the last ten years. It provided a list of experiences that I had, and it gave me the self-confidence to put away my doubts and declare to the universe that I was ready—scared … but ready.

Acknowledgments

First and foremost, I want to thank the authors of each and every book that I read along this journey. I can't image my life without them.

I want to thank all the instructors I named in this book for your hard work and dedication to teaching the intuitive arts. You are amazing!

I want to thank all of my fellow students and seekers for working alongside me in class. I wish you love, light, and much success as we move forward on our individual journeys.

Love and gratitude go out to my mentors at the Learning Light Foundation. To Art Herrera, Terene, and Nick Sutcliffe: thank you for your guidance and support throughout the years.

A special thank you goes out to Shelia Cash, Wendy Leon, Thomas Workman, Dr. Joshua Kai, and Janie Daum, all of whom I met at the end of my journey, for their unconditional friendship and support.

I want to thank my publicist, Virginia Morrel of Balboa Publishing, for sticking with me for almost three years. I started talking to Virginia when I finished an outline for a paranormal thriller (fiction), but I ended up with a creative nonfiction—at least that is what I'm calling this. I also want to thank all the hard workers behind the scenes at Balboa (coordination, editing, design, and marketing) that made this book possible.

I want to thank my fellow writers who inspired me to write this book. To Mary Ellen Gavin, Sarah Schultz, Tye Stewart, and Andrew Oquendo: thank you for listening to my paranormal thriller with an open mind … especially when you found out that I based the main character (a medium) on myself. To Louise E. Gibney, Cal Kraft, and the rest of the gang on Thursday evenings, thank you for helping me overcome my fear of reading the small slices of my life out loud. It made all the difference in the world.

To Stephen King (*On Writing*) and Anne Lamott (*Bird by Bird*) for their incredible books on writing. Thank you! I read both of them while writing this book. I hope I did you proud.

And most importantly, I want to thank my family. To Sydney and Travis, thank you for not outwardly thinking that your Momster was weird. I know it must have been strange when I lectured you about being careful who you invited into our home because of the books on our shelves. I just wasn't sure that your friends' parents would be okay with topics like the tarot, moon spells, charms, and witchcraft. I love you both so much.

To my husband, Kurt, who technically isn't my husband because we are still divorced (*hint*). Thank you for supporting me wholeheartedly while I was writing this book. I honestly thought you were going to talk me out of it, but you didn't. I love and appreciate you so much.

To my furry little one, Lilo "Stitch" Huisman: thank you for being my writing partner. You sat up on the sofa with me at all hours of the day and night while I wrote my thoughts out until my hand hurt. I shall call you my doggy animal guide. What would I do without you?

To my Mom, Dad, and sister Romie, thank you for not judging my path. I know that the conversations were awkward sometimes, but I appreciate you taking the time to listen.

To my brother, Peter, thank you for being my mentor when

you were alive and my guide now that you are in spirit. And thank you for taking me seriously as your little sister. Because of your unconditional love, I have a little more than a smidgen of self-esteem and self-confidence.

To God, my guardian angels, and my spirit guides—and to all the realms of the divine in every dimension of time and space—thank you for your love and support of everyone and everything.

Angel blessings!

Appendix:
My Early Memories

The Queen Mary Ghost

When I was young, my parents took us to southern California every summer for vacation. We jumped into our pale yellow Ford Galaxy 500 and floated down the freeway at 55 miles per hour across the 99-degree desert heat from Arizona to California. This was a yearly event until I was a teenager and no one could stand each other anymore. Our destination was usually Disneyland, Knott's Berry Farm, Magic Mountain (now Six Flags), or the beach.

During one trip in the early 70s, we went to Long Beach to take a tour of the Queen Mary. It is a retired Ocean Liner that, according to Wikipedia, sailed along the Atlantic Ocean from 1936 to 1967. It was enormous. Because my little sister wasn't born yet, I think I was around six years old.

My brother and I got excited seeing it from a distance. We had never been on a boat or ship of any kind before. It was really cool watching it get bigger and bigger as we drove up beside it.

I had a really bad habit of wandering away from my parents. This is a habit that I still have today. The smallest distraction would catch my eye and off I'd go. I lost track of the number of times that I got lost in Kmart. I can still see my mom's face walking toward the front of the store to claim me after hearing, "We have a lost child waiting at checkout number seven," over the loudspeaker. Needless to say, I got it good that night.

We stood in line for a tour as our parents warned us for the fiftieth time to *be good*. Our guide introduced herself, but I don't remember her name. I do remember that she was young and had a good sense of humor. Because I had been marked a wanderer, I had to hold one of my parent's hands at all times. This was really exhausting for both of us. I can honestly say that I know exactly what my dog feels like.

As we walked through the different parts of the ship, I felt like each room had its own personality. Each area *felt* different, and at times, I would feel different too: tired, weak, dizzy, angry, or happy. I also got pounding headaches that would come and go.

And then we entered the Queen Mary's propeller viewing tank. We walked down several flights of thin, metal stairs toward the bottom of the ship. Everything around us was metal. The viewing tank area was eerily dark. It had a small walking path on one side of the twelve-foot-long metal railing that surrounded the tank of ocean water below. I could easily see the giant propeller that was eleven feet under the surface and illuminated by an underwater light. It still gives me chills to this day.

My parents and brother stepped toward the railing to look at it. I was left standing by the stairs that we had just come down. My parents must have been feeling lucky, because they let me loose. A moment later, a handsome man walked up and stood next me. He looked like a navy officer, complete with a hat. Embarrassed, I looked down at the ground and began staring at his white shoes. He knelt down beside me and asked, "Are you enjoying yourself?" Because I considered him a stranger, I didn't want to get into trouble for talking him, so I just nodded my head and went back to staring at the ground.

He stood up at the same time my mom turned around to look at me. "Rena, are you okay?" she asked. I nodded and then glanced over at the man standing to my right. "Who are you talking to?" she asked with confusion in her voice.

Again, I looked up at the man standing to my right and thought, *Technically, I wasn't talking.* He smiled, tilted his hat, and began moving up the stairs. I thought my mom was mad at me for nodding to strangers. Terrified of getting yelled at in front of everyone, I froze and braced myself as she stepped forward to take my hand. She had a really bad habit of pinching me into submission. My arm hurts just thinking about it.

As we continued through the tour, I realized that I was the only one who saw him. (Although, the guide had a weary smile on her face each time she looked at me, so maybe I wasn't *really* the only one.)

Later, my brother, who didn't say a word throughout the entire encounter, told me that there was no one standing next to me. But I knew better.

The Ouija Board

Carla was my neighbor, and she was in junior high. She lived in the house on the corner. Her place was pristine, the yard was perfectly manicured, and the driveway actually glistened in the sun. She was an only child if I remember correctly. We didn't hang out much, only the few times that she was able to come outside with the rest of the neighbor kids. It was my impression that her father didn't approve of us, so he kept her inside where she was safe from our bad influence.

He was an odd man—not tall or attractive, but he was a clean-cut and fit individual. He kept a single chain hung across the base of their driveway. It kept us from riding our bikes onto it for a closer look. It was designed to keep everyone out, including traveling salesmen. My dad used to make it a point to wave at him, but the man always responded with a slight nod and a frown.

One summer afternoon, Carla showed up at our door. "Hi, Rena, do you want to come over and hang out?" she asked. I was shocked. She was a wonderful person, but she was much older and wiser than I was.

"Sure! Let me ask Mom," I said, trying not to kill the moment with too much enthusiasm. It was fine with my mom, so I followed her outside.

"My Dad isn't home; he's at work," she explained on our way up the street. We were greeted by her mother standing in the driveway. She was a nice woman; she was petite with short, brown hair and glasses. Her energy was much lighter than her husband's. Like Carla, she had kind eyes.

It was warm outside, so her mother invited us inside to play. We went in through the side door that entered from the driveway and led straight into the kitchen. As I stepped over the threshold, I could feel the cool, clean air of their home immediately. As my eyes adjusted from being in the bright sunshine, I could see that the light brown cabinets, Formica countertops, and tiled floors were spotless and shiny. Nothing was out of place; it looked unlived in, like a model home. There was no doubt that I could see my reflection in the plastic table cloth. I was really glad that I showered that morning, or I would have been the dirtiest thing in the house.

Carla gave me a quick tour. The living room shelves were filled with books, but what caught my eye was the *Man, Myth & Magic* encyclopedia collection. They were oversized and wrapped in black leather with gold writing. I had seen the commercials for them on TV. They were the Holy Grail of magical information. I couldn't believe it. My eyes widened as I walked toward them slowly in a dream-like state. As I lifted my hand to reach out and touch their smooth surface, I heard Carla's mom shout, "Don't touch those!" Frightened, I jumped and pulled my hands back to my sides. Evidently, the books belonged to Carla's father. "He would know if they were moved," she explained. By this time, Carla's mother looked nervous. I could see it in her body language as she stood there wringing her hands. Carla caught a glance from her mother and led me into her bedroom.

"Rena, have you ever played with a Ouija board before?" she asked. I shook my head from left to right, but when I saw the picture on the box that was sitting on her bed, I was intrigued. The whole idea that I was in her home was so surreal that there was no way I was leaving without playing that game!

Carla explained how the wooden board worked as she removed the pieces from the box. The board was rectangular and displayed the word *yes* in one corner and *no* in the other. The alphabet was written across the middle, and the numbers zero through nine were written below it. There were pictures of a moon and the sun on either side as well. It had an antique look and feel to it.

The only other piece was the planchet. It was ivory-colored plastic in the shape of a long heart, and there was a circle of clear plastic in the middle about an inch wide. There was a metal pin placed in the center of the circle that pointed down toward the board.

As Carla placed the planchet onto the board, she explained how it worked: "To begin, we put the planchet in middle of the board with the top pointing up." I nodded as she continued. "And then we place the tips of our four fingers from both of our hands on each side of the planchet. When we are ready, one of us will ask a question for the *board* to answer." *The board will answer?* I thought.

We were both sitting on the shag carpet and facing each other with the board sitting between us. Carla's mother was standing in the doorway behind me watching. Carla placed the planchet in the middle of the board, and then we gently placed the tips of our fingers onto the planchet. Carla asked the first question that would yield a yes-or-no answer.

The moment she was done, the planchet flew across the board. It moved so fast that I could barely keep my fingers on it. With each question, it flew up to one corner of the board and then back down to the middle, waiting for the next one. They were swift movements, as if someone were holding our wrists. There was no pressure on any part of my fingers, hands, arms, or body. It was as if the energy around us was one with the planchet, connecting us like magnets.

The next few questions required the alphabet. Once again,

Carla asked a question. The planchet moved back and forth across the series of letters and spelled out the answer with incredible speed. When it finally stopped, she looked up behind me at her mother's face, which looked serious.

I lifted my fingers from the planchet and turned to smile at her mother. "That was really fun. Was Carla the one who was moving the planchet?" I asked. They both started to answer at the same time, and they assured me that Carla was not responsible for moving it. Yet they never really explained who was responsible. Before we could continue, her mother looked at her watch, and then, in a slight panic, she explained that I had to leave at once. She practically lifted me up off the floor as she escorted me to the door.

"Carla's father will be home soon; we have to clean up," she said as I walked out the door. I had the very clear impression that I was not allowed in *his* house.

I walked home in a kind of daze with a giant smile on my face, but I kept looking back, worried that Carla's father was going to come around the corner in his truck at any moment and run me over. That was the coolest thing I had ever done, and I couldn't wait to tell my brother.

Unfortunately, I had a big mouth and a huge lapse in judgment because I also shared my awesome adventure with my parents. My mom was fine with it, but my dad nearly had a heart attack.

"You don't know what kind of spirit was moving the planchet," he said with a bead of sweat rolling down his forehead. "Don't ever bring one of those things into the house, Rena. I mean it!" Though valid, his reaction freaked me out. It was confusing and disappointing, but that didn't stop my curiosity. The light was already turned on, and it would take hell and high water to turn it back off.

I'm fairly certain that Carla and her mother knew what I was back then. They already knew what would take decades for me to figure out on my own. I always wondered what might have been if I was able to spend more time with them. Unfortunately, I didn't see Carla much after that—I think her father found out that I was in her home. Still, I will always be grateful to her and her mother for inviting me in that day. And if they knew I was a psychic/medium, it's very likely they were as well.

My Out-of-Body Experience

In junior high, I had a circle of best friends, and we called ourselves the four musketeers. There was Lisa, who lived around the corner; Megan, who ended up marrying Lisa's brother; and Donna, who lived a few streets down.

During high school, we went our separate ways. Lisa, Megan, and Donna went to a local high school in Mesa, Arizona, and I went to Dobson High, a new school in the district that year. Despite the separation, we still kept in touch with occasional phone calls and random meetings at parties.

In 1984, our senior year, Donna had been dating Mark for several years. I heard rumors that they were getting married. On the evening of November 30th, Donna was riding in a car driven by a friend of hers I didn't know. There were four of them. Donna was sitting in the back seat behind the front passenger. The driver of her car made a left turn in front of an oncoming vehicle, and her car was struck. The majority of the impact hit Donna.

The driver of her vehicle and the other two passengers walked away. Donna wasn't so lucky. She was taken to a nearby hospital where she was treated for internal injuries. The accident occurred at eleven in the evening, and Donna passed away at five o'clock the following morning.

I don't remember who told me about the accident, but I remember the impact of the loss of someone who meant so much to me.

Within the week that Donna passed, a viewing was held in a small church. There were hundreds of people who attended. Lisa, Megan, and I went together. When we finally made our way to the front of the line, nothing could prepare us for what we saw. Laid to rest in her coffin, Donna was wearing a wedding dress complete with a veil. We knew that her ex-boyfriend was devastated, but we had no idea that the rumors regarding them getting married were true and that she had purchased a wedding dress. It was shocking, and the sight stunned us into silence.

As the months went by after the funeral, Lisa and I had dreams about Donna. They were so vivid that we both worried that Donna wasn't at rest. And then the strangest thing happened. It was late afternoon on the weekend, about a year and half after Donna's death. I had just come home from running errands all morning. "Hi, Dad," I said as I walked in the side door. He was sitting in his favorite chair watching TV.

"Hi, Rena, how is it going?"

"Good. I just picked up a few things at the store," I said as I walked down the hall to my bedroom.

Before going out later that evening, I decided to take a quick nap. I flopped down on top of my nice, cool bedspread and rested on my back with my hands folded together on top of my stomach. I could hear the birds singing outside my window as I drifted off to sleep.

The next thing I knew, I heard a woman's voice telling me to get up. Groggy, I stood up and tried to regain my balance. The room was dark. *I must have been asleep all day,* I thought. But then I realized that I was standing barefoot on a dirt floor. I reached out to touch the walls, and they were made of dirt too. *Oh my God, I'm underground!*

As the woman continued to speak, I recognized her voice: it was Donna. I turned toward it as my eyes continued to focus. She was standing right in front of me in her wedding dress. But the wedding dress kept fading in and out into regular clothes. I was so happy to see her that I reached out for a hug, but then I remembered that she had passed away and couldn't possibly be standing there.

Where am I? I thought, looking around and trying to figure it out. Meanwhile, Donna continued to talk to me in an almost frantic voice.

She reached out to both of my arms and stood right in front of me in an attempt to keep my attention, but I kept searching for an exit.

"I'm all alone, Rena. Please don't go; please stay with me. I'm scared!" she cried.

Stay where? I thought. I had no idea where we were. Panic was beginning to set in as I looked up and saw a light at the top of the hole we were standing in. It reminded me of an empty well. When I looked closer into the light, I could see the desk where I put on my makeup, the pink walls of my room, my bedroom door that was still open, and the sunlight coming through the window. I could also see my bed and my body lying on top of it, perfectly still, posed in the same way as someone in a casket.

"Oh my God! What is happening? Did I die?" I asked in a whispered panic. I was truly scared. "What is happening? Where are we? How do I get back to my body?" I wanted to grab Donna and shake her into telling me what the hell was going on.

"I need you to stay. Please stay with me. I am all alone and scared," she said while trembling. An overwhelming feeling came over me that I had to make a decision quickly: I could stay with Donna or go back to my body.

"Donna, I can't stay with you. I have to go back; I want to go back!" I explained. Donna began to cry, and that memory still haunts me. She was lonely and scared, and I was going to leave her there by herself. I asked her about the wedding dress and the accident, but I don't remember her response. I remember the *feeling* of the words, but not the words themselves.

Terrified, I knew it was time to return to my body, but I had no idea how to make that happen. I started freaking out and began clawing at the walls. *Maybe I can climb my way out!* And then I heard the sound of my own breath, gasping for air as I sat up in bed covered with sweat. It was like coming up for air from the bottom of the ocean. I jumped off the bed and started looking around the room for a hole in the ground. I then searched for Donna in the closet.

When I didn't find anything, I flew down the hall in three giant steps to my dad who was still sitting in his chair. He looked up to see the panic on my face. "Dad, something just happened while I was sleeping," I said as I stood there shaking. He sat up and turned the volume down on the TV. "Okay, what happened?" he asked.

I let the whole story, detail by detail, roll out of my mouth at a million miles per hour. My arms were waving around in the air and I kept looking back to see whether someone was standing there.

I had heard of OBEs before, and I was pretty sure that my dad had too. But because he was Catholic, this was not a common topic of conversation. As I came to the end of my story, I could see that my dad was perplexed. He knew it was more than just a dream, but he didn't know what advice to give me. I sat down on the sofa staring out into space, and then we both came to the same conclusion: "Pray for her," he said. "If she is a spirit who is lost between both worlds, the one thing that we can do is ask God to find her and take her home so that she isn't lonely anymore." And that is what I did.

My grandmother, Leona, passed away that year as well. I went into my room and prayed to my grandmother: "Hi, Nana, I hope all is going well up in heaven. I need your help. Do you remember Donna? I think she is stuck. Can you please find her and take her to heaven so that she isn't lonely anymore?"

I prayed again that evening, and again the following day. Before I knew it, I couldn't feel Donna around me anymore. I knew in my heart that she had crossed over. She was in the light, no longer caught between this world and the next.

I still have dreams with Donna in them, but I call them visitations. When I am thinking of her or old times, she will come to me in my dreams to give me advice or to let me know that I am not alone. I love it when she does that.

Bibliography

These are some of the books that have influenced me along my path. I hope that you enjoy them as much as I have.

Arroyo, Stephan. *Astrology, Psychology, and the Four Elements: An Energy Approach to Astrology and Its Use in the Counseling Arts.* CRCS Publications, 1978.

Baughman, Alison. *Speaking to Your Soul: Through Numerology.* CreateSpace Independent Publishing Platform, 2013.

Bodine, Echo L. *Relax, It's Only A Ghost.* Element Books Ltd, 2000.

Camp, Ed. Robert. *Cards of Your Destiny: What Your Birthday Reveals About You & Your Past, Present & Future [Paperback] [2004] Reprint.* Sourcebooks, Inc., 2004.

Campbell, Joseph, and Bill Moyers. *The Power of Myth.* Anchor, 1991.

Carter, Mary Ellen, and Harmon H. Bro. *Edgar Cayce: Modern Prophet: Edgar Cayce on Prophecy; Edgar Cayce on Religion and Psychic Experience; Edgar Cayce on Mysteries of the Mind; Edgar Cayce on Reincarnation.* Bonanza Books, 1990.

Cash, Sheila. *Evolve Your Life: Rethink Your Biggest Picture Through Conscious Evolution.* Difference Press, 2015.

Choquette, Sonia. *The Psychic Pathway.* Harmony, 1995.

—. *True Balance: A Commonsense Guide for Renewing Your Spirit.* Harmony, 2000.

—. *Trust Your Vibes: Secret Tools for Six-Sensory Living.* Hay House, 2005.

Cunningham, Scott. *The Truth About Witchcraft Today (Truth About Series).* Llewellyn Publications, 2002.

Dale, Cyndi. *New Chakra Healing: Activate Your 32 Energy Centers.* Llewellyn Publications, 1996.

Désy, Phylameana lila. *The Everything Guide to Reiki: Channel your positive energy to promote healing, reduce stress, and enhance your quality of life.* Adams Media, 2012.

Diane, Ahlquist. *Moon Spells.* Adams Media Corporation, 2002.

Economy, Peter, and Randy Ingermanson. *Writing Fiction For Dummies.* For Dummies, 2009.

Eynden, Rose Vanden. *So you want to be a Medium: A Down to Earth Guide.* Llewellyn Publications, 2006.

Farmer, Steven D. *Animal Spirit Guides: An Easy-to-Use Handbook for Identifying and Understanding Your Power Animals and Animal Spirit Helpers.* Hay House, 2006.

—. *Power Animals: How to Connect with Your Animal Spirit Guide.* Hay House, 2009.

Giesemann, Suzanne R. *The Priest and the Medium: The Amazing True Story of Psychic Medium B. Anne Gehman and Her Husband, Former Jesuit Priest Wayne Knoll, Ph.D.* Hay House, 2009.

Gleason, Yvonne P. *Reiki Journeys: Stories of Personal and Spiritual Growth through Reiki .* Reiki Sanctuary of Northern Virginia, 2014.

Hickey, Isabel M. *Astrology, A Cosmic Science: The Classic Work on Spiritual Astrology.* CRCS Publications, 2011.

Holland, John. *Born Knowing.* Hay House, 2003.

Illes, Judika. *Pure Magic: A Complete Course in Spellcasting.* Weiser Books, 2007.

Jung, C. G., Aniela Jaffe, Clara Winston, and Richard Winston. *Memories, Dreams, Reflections.* Vintage, 1989.

Kai, Dr. Joshua. *The Quantum Prayer: An Inspiring Guide to Love, Healing, and Creating the Best Life Possible*. CreateSpace Independent Publishing Platform, 2015.

King, Stephen. *On Writing: 10th Anniversary Edition: A Memoir of the Craft*. Scribner, 2010.

Lamott, Anne. *Bird by Bird: Some Instructions on Writing and Life*. Anchor, 1995.

Loftus, Myrna. *A Spiritual Approach to Astrology*. Vantage Press, 1980.

Martin, Joel. *We Don't Die: George Anderson's Conversations with the Other Side*. Berkley, 2002.

McMoneagle, Joseph. *Mind Trek*. Crossroad Press, 2014.

—. *The Ultimate Time Machine: A Remote Viewer's Perception of Time, and Predictions for the New Millennium*. Hampton Roads Publishing Company, Inc., 1998.

Myss, Caroline. *Sacred Contracts: Awakening Your Divine Potential*. Harmony, 2003.

Northrop, Suzane. *Second Chance: Healing Messages from the Afterlife*. Jodere Group, 2002.

—. *The Seance: Healing Messages from Beyond (Former Title: Seance: A Guide for the Living)* . Dell Books, 1995.

Ohotto, Robert. *Transforming Fate Into Destiny: A New Dialogue with Your Soul* . Hay House, 2008.

Ph.D., Ph.D. Gary E. Schwartz. *The Afterlife Experiments: Breakthrough Scientific Evidence of Life After Death*. Atria Books, 2003.

Pollack, Rachel. *Seventy-Eight Degrees of Wisdom: A Book of Tarot* . Weiser Books, 2007.

Praagh, James Van. *Ghosts Among Us: Uncovering the Truth About the Other Side*. HarperOne, 2009.

Smith, Gordon. *Intuitive Studies: A Complete Course in Mediumship*. Hay House, 2012.

—. *Spirit Messenger*. Hay House, 2004.

Smith, Philip. *Walking Through Walls*. Atria Books; First Edition edition (September 16, 2008), 2008.

—. *Walking Through Walls: A Memoir*. Atria Books, 2008.

Strunk, William, and E. B. White. *The Elements of Style, Fourth Edition*. Longman, 1999.

Tanner, Wilda B. *The Mystical, Magical, Marvelous World of Dreams*. Wild Comet Publishing LLC, 2004.

Thomson, Sandra A. *Cloud Nine: A Dreamer's Dictionary*. William Morrow Paperbacks, 1999.

—. *The Heart of the Tarot: The Two-card Layout: Easy, Fast, and Insightful*. HarperOne, 2000.

Virtue, Doreen. *Angel Numbers*. Hay House, 2005.

—. *Archangels and Ascended Masters*. Hay House, 2004.

—. *Devine Guidance: How to Have a Dialogue with God and Your Guardian Angels*. Renaissance Books, 1999.

—. *Devine Perscriptions: Spiritual Solutions for You and Your Loved Ones*. Renaissance Books, 2001.

—. *Earth Angels*. Hay House, 2002.

—. *The Lightworkers Way: Awakening Your Spirtual Power To Know And Heal*. Hay House, 1997.

Williams, Lisa. *Life Among the Dead*. Gallery Books, 2009.

Winkowski, Mary Ann. *When Ghosts Speak: Understanding the World of Earthbound Spirits*. Grand Central Publishing, 2009.

Recommended Links

Doreen Virtue: http://www.angeltherapy.com/
Sonia Choquette: http://soniachoquette.net/
John Holland: http://johnholland.com/
Gordon Smith: http://gordonsmithmedium.com/
Steven Farmer: http://www.earthmagic.net/
Vision Quest Books: http://www.visionquestbooks.com/
Amy Brown: http://www.amybrownart.com/
The Learning Light Foundation: http://www.learninglight.org/
Robert Ohotto: http://www.ohotto.com/
A.J. Barrera: http://www.ajbarrera.com/
Hollister Rand: http://www.hollisterrand.com/
James Van Praagh: http://www.vanpraagh.com/
Lisa Williams: http://www.lisawilliams.com/
Hay House: http://www.hayhouse.com/
Alison Baughman: http://visiblebynumbers.com/
JacQuaeline: http://www.intuitionpower.com/
Yvonne P. Gleason: http://www.reikinorthernvirginia.com/
Sheila Cash: http://sheilacash.com/
Joshua Kai: http://makaiolight.com/index.html
Arlington Metaphysical Chapel: http://www.arlingtonmeta.org/
The Monroe Institute: https://www.monroeinstitute.org/
Adult and Community Education Program of Fairfax County
Public Schools: http://www.fcps.edu/is/ace/index.shtml